More Praise for **Seeing Systems**

"*Seeing Systems* offers not just a framework for understanding leadership issues, but practical solutions one can actually implement in an organization."
—Scott Powers, Chief Executive Officer, Old Mutual U.S.

"It is all about relationships. Oshry recognizes this and the importance of organizational dynamics in his works. His insights offer great advice regardless of where you 'sit' in the organization. In fact, you may find that you 'sit' in a different place than you thought."
—Al Grasso, President and Chief Executive Officer, Mitre Corporation

"I have read with enormous interest *Seeing Systems* and must say that through many years of being involved in entities dedicated to systemic understanding, this has been the most exciting reading."
—Dr. Enrique G. Herrscher, Honorary Professor, Universidad de Buenos Aires (UBA), former President, International Society for the Systems Sciences (ISSS)

"Precious few business books reveal know-how that fundamentally changes the way we operate and experience our world of work. *Seeing Systems* helps us grasp what really happens beneath the surface in organizations. Regardless of whether you are an executive, executive coach, middle manager or individual contributor, *Seeing Systems* provides powerful insights and applications for enhancing your effectiveness."
—Julian D. Kaufmann, Vice President, Leadership & Organization Development, Tyco International

"*Seeing Systems* is a much needed antidote to the personal bias that dominates much of our thinking about organizations."
—Timothy J. Giarrusso, Professor, E. Philip Saunders College of Business, Rochester Institute of Technology

"I have been a fan of Oshry's *Seeing Systems* for a number of years and use it extensively to engage staff in recognizing the bigger picture in their everyday activities."
—David Morhart, Deputy Minister of Public Safety and Deputy Solicitor General, Province of British Columbia

"Oshry's work has the power to transform our lives by removing the blinders we usually wear. I regularly used his books and workshops as powerful tools for our senior leaders' development. With great regularity, people reported that they felt liberated and energized once they could see the dances he describes in their personal or professional lives."

—Sabina Nawaz, former Senior Director of Leadership Development, Microsoft, and Principal, Nawaz Consulting LLC

"You never know how students will react to a book, so I wasn't prepared for the electric impact *Seeing Systems* had on the class. They loved it and were clearly affected by its insights and style."

—Barton Kunstler, PhD, Director, Graduate Program in Organizational and Corporate Communications, Emerson College

"We, like fish, are unaware of the medium in which we swim. Oshry takes us to a higher level, allowing us to see the systemic ocean that engulfs us. From this viewpoint, we can change the very nature of how we swim. The perspective about systems, power, and relationships hits the reader clearly and with impact. This book can make a difference in our organizations, and in our lives."

—Thomas Crum, author of *The Magic of Conflict*, *Journey to the Center*, and *Three Deep Breaths*

"*Seeing Systems* is exactly what happened for me the first time I read Oshry's work. This was the first organizational model that made sense of what I was experiencing as a manager. Not a simple laundry list of ideas or 'paradigms' but practical theories based on how people behave in the workplace. I applied Oshry's principles daily as a manager of a county jail in Washington, and I continue to apply them, in my retirement, managing large volunteer organizations."

—Lucia Meijer, former Administrator, King County North Rehabilitation Facility

"Oshry's framing of systems and the interaction between functions and levels is dead on. *Seeing Systems* is a close friend for everyone on our team."

—Rob Kramer, Director, Training and Development, University of North Carolina

"Oshry weaves a remarkable explanation for the subtle, and largely unseen, ways in which our structures influence our behavior. Part poetry, part philosophy, part practical advice, this book offers a creative lens for examining our own behavior."

—Marvin Weisbord, Co-Director, Future Search Network; coauthor of *Future Search*; and author of *Productive Workplaces Revisited*

"Anyone who is in the business of leading others or managing change will profit from the lenses *Seeing Systems* offers. They help us understand and avoid the all too common traps of disempowerment and failed partnerships. Instead of blaming others, ourselves, or the system, we learn how these organizational dynamics predictably shape our perceptions in ways that are self-defeating, and we see how we can rise above them and create relationships and organizations where collaboration can flourish."

—Dr. Gervase R. Bushe, Segal Graduate School of Business, Simon Fraser University, author of *Clear Leadership* and coauthor of *Parallel Learning Structures*

"Oshry is a genius in designing simulations of complex social systems and in constructing frameworks that generate rare insights into the simplicity that lies beyond the complexity of such systems. For systems that have a large group of employees that consider themselves to be disempowered—whether factory line workers, government bureaucrats, or orchestra musicians—*Seeing Systems* offers the most powerful tools I know."

—Grady McGonagil, EdD, Director of Learning, Generon Consulting

"Oshry explains in clear, convincing, and poetic language why people behave as they do in organizational life. His insights shine a bright light into the dark cave of organizational systems…and show us a way out."

—Jeffrey and Merianne Liteman, coauthors of *Retreats that Work*

"*Seeing Systems* helped me better understand my many roles; it also yielded valuable insights into the worlds of those in other positions, enabling me to adjust my behavior in ways that make me a more effective leader and follower. The book has made a lasting impression."

—Jeffrey B. Cooper, PhD, Director, Biomedical Engineering, Partners HealthCare System, Inc.

Barry Oshry

Seeing Systems

Unlocking the Mysteries of Organizational Life

BERRETT-KOEHLER PUBLISHERS, INC.
San Francisco

Berrett-Koehler Publishers, Inc.
235 Montgomery Street, Suite 650
San Francisco, CA 94104-2916
Tel: (415) 288-0260   Fax: (415) 362-2512   www.bkconnection.com

Ordering Information
Quantity sales. Special discounts are available on quantity purchases by corporations, associations, and others. For details, contact the "Special Sales Department" at the Berrett-Koehler address above.
Individual sales. Berrett-Koehler publications are available through most bookstores. They can also be ordered directly from Berrett-Koehler: Tel: (800) 929-2929; Fax: (802) 864-7626; www.bkconnection.com
Orders for college textbook/course adoption use. Please contact Berrett-Koehler: Tel: (800) 929-2929; Fax: (802) 864-7626.
Orders by U.S. trade bookstores and wholesalers. Please contact Ingram Publisher Services, Tel: (800) 509-4887; Fax: (800) 838-1149;
E-mail: customer.service@ingrampublisherservices.com; or visit www.ingrampublisherservices.com/Ordering for details about electronic ordering.

Berrett-Koehler and the BK logo are registered trademarks of Berrett-Koehler Publishers, Inc.

Printed in the United States of America

Berrett-Koehler books are printed on long-lasting acid-free paper. When it is available, we choose paper that has been manufactured by environmentally responsible processes. These may include using trees grown in sustainable forests, incorporating recycled paper, minimizing chlorine in bleaching, or recycling the energy produced at the paper mill.

Library of Congress Cataloging-in-Publication Data
Oshry, Barry, 1932-
  Seeing systems : unlocking the mysteries of organizational life / Barry Oshry. -- 2nd ed.
      p. cm.
  Includes bibliographical references.
  ISBN 978-1-57675-455-9 (pbk. : alk. paper)
  1. Social systems. 2. Organizational behavior. 3. Management. I. Title.

HM701.O855 2007
302.3'5--dc22   2007010751

Second Edition
17 16 15 14 13 12   18 17 16 15 14 13 12 11 10 9

Dianne Platner, book design and production; Kristie Hines, copyeditor; Debra Gates, proofreader; Eric Taros, illustrator.

For Karen

Contents

Act II. Seeing Patterns of Relationship   61

Act III. Seeing Patterns of Process 129

Scene 1. Process Blindness 131

Scene 2. From Process Blindness to Process Sight 139

Scene 3. The Politics of System Processes 183

Preface to the Second Edition

The offer to write a second edition is a gift to the author—a chance to correct errors that became obvious the moment the first edition came to print and an opportunity to clarify points, to respond to critics, to answer readers' questions and, if possible, respond to their requests, and to deepen the work based on what has been learned in the ten intervening years. For readers of the first edition, rest assured, the old favorites are here—from Pinball to the Dance of Blind Reflex, the He/She dialogues, earthworms and slugs, and the Dance of the Robust System. And there is much that is new: new cases, a new Power Lab story, a deepened exploration into the Dance of Blind Reflex, and a new section on Uncertainty and the Tunnel of Limited Options.

This second edition has given me the opportunity to continue the exploration into the human and system costs of system blindness and the new level of humanity that comes to us with system sight. This was a gift to me, and I trust that it is a gift to the reader as well.

Prologue: Overcoming System Blindness

Top, Middle, Bottom, and Customer:

Positions and Conditions

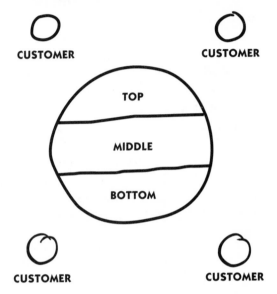

Throughout this book, we will be talking about Tops, Middles, Bottoms, and Customers. Given the complexity of organizations, this may appear to be a gross simplification of organizational life as the reader has experienced it. At times, as in "A Familiar Story" (which follows), we will treat these as *positions:* you are either a Top or a Middle or a Bottom or a Customer. At other times we will treat these as *conditions* all of us face in whatever position we occupy. In certain interactions we are Top, having overall responsibility for some piece of the action; in other interactions we are Bottom, on the receiving end of initiatives over which we have no control. In other interactions we are Middle, caught between conflicting demands and priorities. And in still other interactions, we are Customer, looking to some other person or group for a product or service we need. So, even in the most complex, multilevel, multifunctional organizations, we are all constantly moving in and out of Top/Middle/Bottom/Customer conditions.

A Familiar Story of Tops, Middles, Bottoms, and Customers

There is a pattern that develops with great regularity in the wide variety of organizations and institutions. The pattern goes something like this:

Tops are burdened by what feels like unmanageable complexity;
Bottoms are oppressed by what they see as distant and uncaring Tops;
Middles are torn and confused between the conflicting demands and priorities coming at them from Tops and Bottoms;
Customers feel done-to by nonresponsive delivery systems.

Top "teams" are caught up in destructive turf warfare;
Middle peers are alienated from one another, noncooperative and competitive;
Bottom group members are trapped in stifling pressures to conform.

Tops are fighting fires when they should be shaping the system's future;
Middles are isolated from one another when they should be working together to coordinate system processes;
Bottoms' negative feelings toward Tops and Middles distracts them from putting their creative energies into the delivery of products and services;
Customers' disgruntlement with the system keeps them from being active partners in helping the system produce the products and services they need.

Throughout the system there is personal stress, relationship breakdowns, and severe limitations in the system's capacity to do what it intends to do.

When this pattern develops, our tendency is to explain it in terms of the character, motivation, and abilities of the individuals involved—*that's just the way* they *are*—or in terms of the specific nature of one's organization—*that's just the way* we *are*. If our explanations are personal, then our solutions are also personal: fix the players, fire them, rotate them, divorce them. If our explanations are specific to our organization, then we fix the organization: reorganize, reengineer, restructure.

What I intend to demonstrate in this book is that this pattern is neither personal nor specific to any given organization. It is systemic. And because *systemic* is such a pervasive, multiple-meaning term, let me clarify its use here.

We humans are systems creatures. Our consciousness—how we experience ourselves, others, our systems, and other systems—is shaped by the structure and processes of the systems we are in. As a single example, when Tops are involved in turf warfare, this is less likely to be a personal issue—much as it may seem like that to the participants—than a systemic one, a vulnerability that develops with remarkable regularity in the Top world; therefore, to deal with turf issues as a personal issue is to miss the point entirely. This is true of many of the other "personal" issues in organizational life as well.

There is a tendency to resist this notion; we prefer seeing ourselves as captains of our own ships; we prefer the notion that we believe what we believe and think what we think because of *who* we are, not *where* we are. I will demonstrate how such thinking is the costly illusion of system blindness—an illusion that results in needless stress, destructive conflicts, broken relationships, missed opportunities, and diminished system effectiveness. And this blindness has its costs in all the systems of our lives—in our families, organizations, nations, and ethnic groups.

My purpose in this book is to transform system blindness into system sight. The paradox is this: With system sight we *can* become captains of our own ships as we understand the nature of the waters in which we sail.

We Are Social Systems Creatures

We humans spend our lives in systems:
in the family,
the classroom,
the friendship group,
the team,
the organization,
the task force,
the faith group,
the community,
the bowling league,
the nation,
the ethnic group.
We find joy
and sadness,
exhilaration
and despair,
good relationships
and bad ones,
opportunities
and frustrations.
So much happens to us in system life,
yet system life remains a mystery.

When We Don't See Systems

When we don't see systems,
we fall out of the possibility of partnership with one another;
we misunderstand one another;
we make up stories about one another;
we have our myths and prejudices about one another;
we hurt and destroy one another;
we become antagonists when we could be collaborators;
we separate when we could remain together happily;
we become strangers when we could be friends;
we oppress one another when we could live in peace;
and our systems—organizations, families, task forces, faith
groups—squander much of their potential.
All of this happens without awareness or choice—
dances of blind reflex.

Five Types of System Blindness:
Spatial, Temporal, Relational, Process, and Uncertainty

We suffer from Spatial Blindness.
We see our part of the system
but not the whole;
we see what is happening with us
but not what is happening elsewhere;
we don't see what others' worlds are like,
the issues they are dealing with,
the stresses they are experiencing;
we don't see how our world impacts theirs
and how theirs impacts ours;

we don't see how all the parts influence one another.
In our spatial blindness,
we fail to understand one another,
we develop stereotypes of one another,
we take personally much that is not personal,
and, as a consequence, many potentially productive
contributions are lost to the system.

We suffer from Temporal Blindness.
We see the present
but not the past;
we know what we are experiencing now
but not what has led to these experiences;
we know our satisfactions and frustrations,
our feelings of closeness and distance,
the issues and choices and challenges we are currently facing.
All of this we experience in the present
but we don't see the history of the present,
the story of our system that has brought us to this point in
time.
In our temporal blindness,
we misdiagnose the current situation,
and in our efforts to solve system problems
we fix what doesn't need to be fixed
and fail to fix what does.

We suffer from Relational Blindness.
In systems, we exist only in *systemic* relationship to one
another:

We are in Top/Bottom relationships,
sometimes as Top and sometimes as Bottom;

we are in End/Middle/End relationships;
sometimes as Middle torn between two or more Ends,
and sometimes as one of several Ends tearing at a common
Middle;

we are in Provider/Customer relationships,
sometimes as Provider and sometimes as Customer;

we are sometimes a member of the Dominant culture in
which there are the Others,
and sometimes we are the Other within the Dominant
culture.

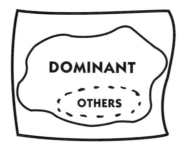

We tend not to see ourselves in these systemic relationships,
nor do we see the dances we fall into in these relationships:
Becoming Burdened Tops
and Oppressed Bottoms,
Disappointed Ends
and Torn Middles,
Judged Providers
and Done-to Customers,
the Righteous Dominants
and the Righteous Others.
In our relational blindness,
we experience much personal stress and pain,
potential partnerships fail to develop,
and system contributions are lost.

We suffer from Process Blindness.
We don't see our systems as wholes,
as entities in their environment.
We don't see the processes of the whole
as the whole struggles to survive.

We don't see how "It" differentiates
in an environment of shared responsibility and complexity
and how we fall into Turf Warfare with one another.
We don't see how "It" individuates
in a diffusing environment
and how we become alienated from one another.
We don't see how "It" coalesces
in an environment of shared vulnerability
and how we become enmeshed in GroupThink with one
another.
In our process blindness,
our relationships with our peers deteriorate,
productive partnerships fail to develop,
and our contributions to the system suffer.

When we suffer from Uncertainty Blindness,
we see fixed positions battling fixed positions,
but we don't see the uncertainty underlying these positions,
the conditions for which there are no obviously correct
answers;
in our positional blindness,
we escape from uncertainty into certainty,
from mystery into fixed unassailable positions about
how to manage our responsibility in the Top world,
our vulnerability in our Bottom world,
our tearing in our Middle world,
our coming together in a world of Dominants and Others.
In our uncertainty blindness,
our righteous battles with one another keep us from
realizing our full potential as Tops, Middles, Bottoms, and
Dominants and Others.

Seeing Systems

This book is about seeing systems.

It is about overcoming system blindness.

It is about seeing our part in the context of the whole in ways that enable us to avoid misunderstandings and to interact more productively across organizational lines (Act One).

It is about seeing the present in the context of the past, such that we can get a more accurate picture of our current condition (Act One).

It is about seeing ourselves in relationship with others and creating satisfying and productive partnerships in these relationships (Act Two).

It is about seeing our systems' processes in ways that enable us to create systems with extraordinary capacities for surviving and developing (Act Three).

It is about seeing the uncertainties in our system conditions in ways that enable us to move past the destructive battles of righteous position versus righteous position (Act IV).

My Windows into Systems:
The Power Lab and The Organization Workshop

■

THE POWER LAB

The Elite (Tops)

Managers (Middles)

and Immigrants (Bottoms)

Living Together in the Community of New Hope

My understanding of systems is a fortuitous outcome of work that had another goal. Over thirty-five years ago, I set out to create a learning environment in which people could deepen their understanding of power and powerlessness in social systems. The result was the Power Lab.[1]

The basic idea was to create a societal setting in which people could experience issues of power and powerlessness directly and dramatically. And so we created a world with clear-cut differences in power and resource control—a world somewhat ironically called the Community of New Hope.

There are three social classes in New Hope—the Elite (or Tops), who control the society's wealth and institutions; the Managers (or Middles), who manage the society's institutions for the Elite; and the Immigrants (or Bottoms), who enter the society with no funds, few resources, and no control over the society's institutions. This new world is compelling in that it encompasses all aspects of participants' lives—the quality of their housing and meals, the job opportunities available to them, the amount of money they have, their access to resources, and more.

A good play needs an appropriate theater, and we were fortunate early on to discover the Craigville Conference Center on Cape Cod.[2] Craigville offered an isolated setting with a variety of housing possibilities for the various social classes and a huge tabernacle that could house the society's institutions—its court, newspaper, company store, employment center, pub, and theater. And most important, the Craigville staff have over the years functioned as patient, understanding, cooperative, and sometimes bemused partners in this venture.

The staff members create the "world" into which participants are "born"—as either Elite, Managers, or Immigrants—and then step back and allow the community to unfold. There are no scenarios to follow, no further directions from staff. What becomes of the society depends on whatever the collection of players makes of it.

The Power Lab was created to support participants in their learning about systems and power, but I have undoubtedly been its major beneficiary. Over the past thirty-five years, I have played a variety of roles in these Communities of New Hope, sometimes as an active player—Elite, Manager, or Immigrant—but more often as an Anthropologist standing outside the system, collecting its history as it unfolds, observing and interviewing societal members. It was not until several years had passed that I realized what a remarkable situation I had fallen into. How often does one have the opportunity to stand outside a social system and observe its total life—to be privy to the separate deliberations of each class as well as to their interactions with one another?

Several of the scenes to follow come directly from the Power Labs (**14**, Bart and Barb; **15**, "'Anthropology' or Mick Gets Wiped Out"; **26**, "Daniel: Mutant in the Middle Space"; **45**, "Alienation Among the Middles"; **50**, "Immigrant Martha Has a Breakdown"; and **66**, "A Mutant Moment in the Middle"), and these scenes are but the tip of the iceberg. Everything in this book is infused with learning drawn from the Power Labs.

The reader may be taken aback by two stories of personal breakdown at the Power Lab. The Power Lab *is* a challenging experience, and participants are cautioned to that effect prior to enrolling. On the other hand, the Power Lab is probably a more supportive environment than most of our other organizational and institutional environments: All participants have their own personal coach who works with them before, during, and after the program; additionally, there are periodic Times Out of Time (TOOT) sessions in which participants can pull back from the experience and gain perspective on it. Still, there were these two breakdowns. Both were "cured" before the lab ended, in ways that enlightened all of us, and in both cases the "breakdown" and its "cure" were clearly systemic, although on the surface the breakdowns appeared to be personal. These two stories offer important lessons about the systemic nature of apparently personal breakdowns in the wider world.

■

THE ORGANIZATION WORKSHOP

Tops (Executives)

Middles (Managers)

Bottoms (Workers)

Customers

Working Together in Creative Consultants, Inc. (CCI)

The Organization Workshop is an offshoot of the Power Lab. People who participated in the Power Labs began to request that we bring our work into their organizations. Apart from a few truly adventurous souls, most organizations were reluctant to do a full-scale Power Lab in-house. However, there was considerable interest in helping executives, managers, and workers deepen their understanding of systems and their ability to work cooperatively with one another. This interest set the stage for the development of the Organization Workshop.

Again, the educational strategy is to create a learning environment or stage on which participants can directly experience key processes and dilemmas of organizational life. In this workshop, participants are "born" into an organization that exists for between a few hours and a day. The organization—CCI—is composed of Executives (Tops), who have overall responsibility for the system, and a group of Managers (Middles) responsible for Worker groups (Bottoms) whose members work on various projects assigned by Tops or Middles; outside the organization are potential Customers who have projects they need help on and money to pay for services. Staff simply set the stage; we put people into position, present the traditions of the organization, then step back and turn the organization loose.

In each workshop, there are Times Out of Time (TOOTs; see **10** and 11), in which we stop the organization, bring everyone together, and have them describe their experiences as Tops, Middles, Bottoms, and Customers. What are their worlds like? What pressures are they experiencing? How does each part of the system experience the other parts? These TOOTs tend to be incredibly illuminating experiences for participants. But consider for a moment what a remarkable learning opportunity the TOOTs have been for me—listening to many hundreds of people over the years as they describe their experiences as Tops, Middles, Bottoms, and Customers. For me, what a light this has shed on the nature of systems! And my intention in this book is to share that light with you.

Swimmers, Slugs, and Ballet Notes: A Word About Style

As you may have already noticed, this book is written in a nontraditional form. There are acts and scenes, pinballs and talking body parts and mysterious "swimmers"; there are poems and dialogues along with conceptual material and cases; there are amebocytes and slugs and earthworms, a variety of dances, and even one set of ballet notes. The imagery of dance is used regularly because so many system processes seem balletic in nature: One party pulls up responsibility to himself or herself while the other passes it up; Bottom groups neatly and regularly split into the "reasonables" versus the "hardliners"; Middles fly apart from one another while Bottoms coalesce. There is form and coherence and predictability to all of these movements. None of which is to imply a lightness to these dances because the dances I describe alienate us from one another, knock us out of the possibility of partnership, and sometimes lead to wholesale death and destruction.[3]

Theater, too, in its various forms, has played an important part in my work. Theater enables us to bring into play a variety of senses: We can see the action, hear it, feel it, dance to it, and join in with it. The Power Lab and the Organization Workshop are forms of organizational improvisation theater: beginning conditions are created, participant-actors enter the stage, and, without further instruction, they improvise. *The Terrible Dance of Power* has had several staged performances, as has *The Dance of Disempowerment.*[4] *The Dance of the Robust System* (**62**) still awaits it first performance. More recently, staged performance and interactive theater have been added to our Seeing Systems repertoire.

It is my fondest wish that you are enriched by the diversity of formats provided in this book and that the various pieces come together to help you see more clearly the many systems of which you are a part. My wish is that through your seeing systems in more depth, system life will become richer and more meaningful for you; you will have a deeper understanding of your experiences in systems; you will see new strategies for making happen what you want to have happen and what your systems need to have happen; and you will discover ways to create systems that contribute to the world and are deeply satisfying to you and other system members.

Acknowledgments

I offer my thanks to some very special people who, over the years, through their encouragement, confrontation, support, and challenge, have contributed to this volume. To Steven Piersanti, for his continuing support and encouragement while gently yet unrelentingly urging me toward deeper levels of exploration. I am grateful to the Brookline Group—Lee Bolman, Dave Brown, Tim Hall, Todd Jick, Adam Kahane, Bill Kahn, and Phil Mirvis—some of whom (I for one) have been meeting monthly for over twenty-five years to nourish, comfort, and prod one another toward greater self-awareness and personal and professional growth. The Power + Systems E-Team and Power Lab staffs, past and present, have been a inspiration, demonstrating the possibilities of high-commitment learning and performance teams. I am buoyed by the hundreds of Organization Workshop trainers who are carrying this work to organizations and institutions around the globe. Warner Burke and Vlad Dupre offered unwavering support for my early, formative, and not always elegant work during their tenures at the National Training Laboratories. Mike McNair, Perviz Randeria, Leigh Wilkinson, and Barry Johansen provided critical readings of early drafts of this book. I thank Edwin Mayhew for a delightful collaborative relationship as we developed workshop designs that led to the Organization Workshop, Fritz Steele and Joe Meier for our partnership during the early days of the Power Lab, and Bob DuBrul for his pioneering work in putting Middle Integration theory into practice. The entire staff of the Craigville Conference Center—housekeeping, kitchen, grounds, directors, and front office—has worked diligently with us since 1972 to create the environment in which Power Labs have flourished. I have been blessed by unstinting love from my daughters, Leslie Perreault and Karen Kennedy, whose estimates of my abilities have far exceeded my own and have therefore given me high standards to aim for. A deep bow of admiration, gratitude, and love to Karen Ellis Oshry, my partner in all aspects of life, who has labored mightily by my side, tolerating my moods and reading and critiquing more variations of this work than any human being should ever be made to endure. And finally, I am indebted to the many thousands of people who have participated in our Power Labs and Organization Workshops and who have allowed me to be with them, observe them, and interview them as they wrestled with the challenges of system life. They came to me as students, but so much of the contents of this book I have learned from them.

As the Talmud says: From all my teachers I have learned. I thank you all for your contributions yet hold none of you responsible for the contents of this work.

Barry Oshry
Boston, Massachusetts
February 2007

SEEING THE BIG PICTURE

Act I

Seeing the Part Without the Whole

Generally, if we are paying attention, we know what life is like for us in our part of the system. Other parts of the system are, for the most part, invisible to us. We do not know what others are experiencing, what their worlds are like, what issues they are dealing with, what dilemmas they are facing, what stresses they are undergoing. To makes matters worse, sometimes we *think* we know when in fact we do not. We have our beliefs, myths, and prejudices, which we accept as the truth and which become the bases of our actions. This blindness to other parts of the system—which we call *spatial blindness*—is a source of considerable misunderstanding, conflict, and diminished system contribution.

Seeing the Present Without Seeing the Past

Temporal blindness refers to the fact that all current events in system life have a history; there is a coherent tale that has led to this particular point in time. Generally that history is invisible to us. We experience the present but are blind to the complex set of events that have brought us to the present. And again, it is this blindness to the history of the moment that is a source of considerable misunderstanding and conflict.

Scene 1 describes the consequences of spatial and temporal blindness.
Scene 2 and 3 deal with the transformation of spatial blindness into spatial sight and temporal blindness into temporal sight.

Scene 1
When We Don't See the Big Picture

1 Pinball

Sometimes life in the organization feels like a game of pinball,
and we're the little metal ball.
We start each day launched into a mysterious world of
bumpers
lights
bells
and whistles.
Lights flash on
and off.
Buzzers sound.
Gates open
and close,
sometimes propelling us at high speed to some other center
of the action,
and sometimes letting us drop quietly
into a hole.

All of this is a mystery to us.
Is this just a set of random events?

Or is there some grand scheme
known to others, but not to us?
One day we hit a bumper.
Lights flash.
Bells ring.
Big numbers go up on the scoreboard.
The next day we keep an eye out for that bumper.
We hit it.
Nothing. A dull thud.
And we continue, puzzled, along our way.

Some days there's lots of action
and big scores.
Other days there's lots of action
but not much of a score to show for it.
And other days there's very little of either.
At the end of the day—
lots of action
or little,
high scores
or low—
we drop through the final gate, heading home.
Sometimes we're impressed with our accomplishments,
sometimes depressed by our failures,
sometimes we're dreading the next launch,
sometimes we're champing at the bit for the next game.
And most times,
as we slide past the gate heading home,
we pause momentarily to reflect:

NOW WHAT WAS THAT ALL ABOUT?

2 The Manager of the Heart

Suggestion: *You might enjoy reading this piece to a group of supervisors or middle managers; see if they know what it is like to be "The Manager of the Heart."*

Life in the organization may feel like a game of pinball,
but the organization itself works more like the human body,
everything neatly connected to everything else.
However, when we don't see the whole,
it can all feel like one chaotic mess.
Take the Manager of the Heart.

At times it's a peaceful job.
A nice even supply of fresh blood comes in from the lungs.
All engines pump smoothly: Lub . . . dub . . . lub . . . dub.

Oh-oh! EMERGENCY! EMERGENCY!
Bells ring.
Buzzers sound.
Messengers come bursting into your office:
chemical messengers from the bloodstream,
electrical messengers from nerve endings.
Who are these guys? Where do they get their information?
Who gives them the authority to tell you what to do?
"What emergency?" you ask. "Where?"
"THERE'S NO TIME TO EXPLAIN!" say the Big Shot
Messengers.
"JUST START SOME HEAVY PUMPING!"
So you tell your people: "FULL AHEAD ON THE
PUMPS!"

You've got a good crew;
in no time they've got those pumps working away at full capacity:
LUB . . . DUB . . . LUB . . . DUB.
You're proud of your crew. You turn to those Messengers and say:
"OK. Bring on that emergency. We can handle anything!"
But the Messengers aren't looking at you;
they're checking their pagers.
"Forget it," says the electrical messenger.
"Cut back," says the chemical messenger.
"Emergency's canceled," they say.
Emergency's canceled? We're just getting up a head of steam.
"CUT BACK! CUT BACK!" They're desperate now.
"YOU'LL BURST SOME PIPES!"
"What'll I tell my crew?"
"CUT BACK!!!!"

So you tell your crew.
"It's for the good of the system," you tell them.
"What do you want from me?" you ask them.
"I don't make the rules around here."

And then it's calm again.
A nice even flow of blood.
Pumps humming along: Lub . . . dub . . . lub . . . dub.
And you start thinking.

You start worrying about your crew.
How many changes of direction can these folks take?
Will I be able to count on them in a real emergency?

You start thinking about those Messengers,
those Specialists,
acting like big shots,
giving out orders,
all that technical mumbo jumbo.
When was the last time any of them bloodied their hands
opening and closing a stuck valve?

You start thinking about the Bigwigs.
Whoever they are,
wherever they are,
are they just playing games with us or what?
Maybe they know what they're doing,
maybe they don't.
What do they do up there all day anyhow?
Maybe they've got the big picture,
but what if they don't?
What if they're just . . . crazy?

And then you start thinking about yourself:
All this stress,
the way you blew up at those Messengers.
They're just doing their jobs after all.
Maybe you're losing your cool.
Maybe you can't cut it anymore.
Maybe you're not half the heart you used to be.

Oh-oh! What's that sound?
Who's that racing along the bloodstream?
I know, I know.

EMERGENCY! EMERGENCY!

3 | The Mystery of the Swim

We may not see the big picture, but that doesn't stop us from creating our own version of it.

In John Barth's "Night-Sea Journey," a "swimmer" tells us of his journey.[1] He is the sole survivor of what began as a horde of eager, strong, and dedicated swimmers—thousands of them, millions, maybe billions! (He's not sure how many there were.) Only he remains—exhausted and confused. The others are gone, drowned in what now seems like an endless and pointless misadventure. Some, disillusioned and hopeless, have taken their own lives.

Along the way, there were many debates among the swimmers. What was this journey about? When did it begin? Where would it end? What purpose, if any, did it serve?

Different camps with competing philosophies developed regarding the meaning of the night-sea journey. Some argued that there was no meaning to it, that it was a pointless venture, that the struggles and deaths of the swimmers were all in vain. Many from this school took their own lives out of despair.

Others believed that the meaning of the venture lay in the swim itself, that the point of the swim was to swim as best as one could for as long as one could.

Still others believed that the swim was part of some grand design that they, the swimmers, could only speculate about but never fully comprehend.

Within the grand design school, there were varying viewpoints: Some believed that the grand design was inherently good, others believed it was evil, and others believed it was neither good nor evil but that it merely existed.

But now all the others are gone; the debates, the discussions, the schools of philosophy have all drowned in the night sea. Only the narrator remains. We listen to him tell of his journey; he shares his thoughts and feelings. He is tired and confused. Should he continue the struggle or, like the others, allow himself to drown?

And as we read on, we too are confused and discomfited. The swimmer's story is an unsatisfactory one for us. The questions that plague him plague us too. What *is* this night-sea journey? Where did it begin? Where will it end? What purpose, if any, does it serve? The swimmer tells us in great detail about *his* journey, yet that is not enough for us. We need to comprehend the journey itself, the whole of which he is but a component part.

Barth never gives us the answer we seek, and without that answer, the journey remains for us an unsettling mystery.

However, if, during our reading—the first, second, or third time through—it comes to us what this night-sea journey is, we are struck with great illumination. Now, having grasped the whole, we read the story through again. What once was confusing is now crystal clear; what once seemed complex and mysterious is now simple and straightforward. The squabbles, debates, and philosophical discussions all make sense to us. *And they all seem like so much silly superstition.*[2]

■　　■　　■

Barth's tale is both a sly joke and a challenging message. He is less concerned with those night-sea swimmers than with us and—given our remarkable brains—our apparently unlimited capacity to create stories that explain what we really don't know. We are story-making machines; we have stories explaining everything from the mystery of life to why the boss never responded to our memo. If we realized that we were making up stories, there'd be some fun to the process and little damage. The problem comes when we believe that our stories are the truth, and we then act on the basis of that "truth."

The challenge is to be able to move past our local picture and the imperfect "truths" it generates to seeing the larger picture and the truths it reveals. First, let's look at how it usually goes—*not always, not with everyone, but with great regularity*—when, in our spatial blindness, we see the part but not the whole.

4 Seeing the Local Picture

Some systems are perfectly healthy
when viewed from the perspective of the whole;
but when viewed from the perspective of any one part,
they appear to be disorganized, chaotic, a collection of
random events.

Our Heart Manager didn't have the big picture.

All she knew about was what was happening in her small
piece of the system.

All she knew directly was that decisions affecting her were
being made in some remote power center.

She didn't know how those decisions were being made
and she didn't know whether to trust them.

She felt beleaguered by interference from a variety of staff
specialists.

She was concerned with potential labor unrest among her
troops,
who also did not have the big picture.

She was beset by rumors.

There was talk of a shutdown in the stomach during the
emergency.

Was it true? What did it mean? Would the heart be next?

For our Heart Manager, system life was a game of pinball.

When we have a local perspective:

- Things seem a lot messier than they really are or they seem a lot neater than they really are.
- We tend to blame ourselves for things that may not be our fault or we blame others for things that may not be their fault.
- We react to rumors rather than facts.
- We tend to misinterpret events happening elsewhere in the system.

- We tend to misunderstand and misjudge others in the system:

  We may see them as malicious, incompetent, and insensitive when in fact they are not.

  We may see them as well-meaning and all-wise when in fact they are not.

- We are unsure about ourselves, about what to do, about how our actions fit in with the actions of others and with the whole.

When we have a local perspective, organizational life feels like

a game

of pinball . . . or worse.

5 "Stuff" Happens

We may be blind to others' worlds,

but this does not stop them from sending "stuff" our way.

Here you are going about your business

 - - - - - **YOU**

and then . . .

stuff happens.

Some of the stuff that comes our way is positive, surprisingly

good news:

- We get the bonus we've been waiting for.
- The project is accepted.

Some of the stuff that comes our way is noxious:

- We don't like it.

Some of the stuff that comes our way is a mystery:

- "Why on earth are they doing that?"

And some of the stuff that comes our way is both—

noxious and a mystery.

For example, you make what seems like a simple request of your supervisor, and instead of saying, "Sure thing, you can count on it, it's coming your way," your supervisor looks at his feet, shuffles around, and mumbles, "Uh . . . well . . . let's see . . . er . . . well, I'll see what I can do." The supervisor's reaction is stuff coming your way. Noxious and a mystery. And you react: *It was just a simple request! Where do they get these weak wishy-washy supervisors?*

You go to your workers with a proposal you think they will be enthusiastic about, and instead, they put up a wall of resistance. Their resistance is stuff heading your way. Noxious and a mystery. And your reaction: *I just don't get it; what is the matter with these people?*

You know that your customer is upset, so you make a gesture to soothe the customer's feelings, and instead of appreciation, the customer replies with anger and sarcasm. More stuff heading your way. And your reaction: *How did these customers get to be so nasty?*

You send a memo to your Top Executive, making what you feel are valuable suggestions for improving the operation. Weeks go by, and there is no response to your memo. More stuff. (Physicists would probably refer to this as "minus stuff.") And you react: *Those Tops, they talk the talk, but don't walk the walk.*

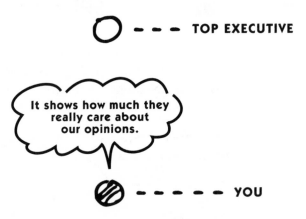

So stuff comes at us regularly—noxious stuff, mysterious stuff, minus stuff. And how do we react to stuff (*not always, not everyone, but with great regularity*)?

1. *We make up stories that explain the stuff.* Our brains don't like mysteries, so in the absence of knowledge about other people's worlds, we quickly fill the void with our stories about them. We create our

myths about their motives, and because we don't see ourselves making up stories, we see our stories as the truth.

2. *We evaluate others.* In our stories, we see them as malicious, insensitive, or incompetent.

3. *We take the stuff personally.* We experience it as if it is aimed at us and intended to hurt or block us.

4. *We react to the stuff.* We get mad, we get even, we withdraw.

5. *We lose focus.* If we had started off with some good intention, we quickly lose interest in that good intention, and instead our focus is on the stuff, our stories about what lies behind the stuff, and our emotions.

6. Our actions then become the stuff for others. They make up their myths about us—about *our* motives and competencies. They take our actions personally and react to us—getting mad, getting even, withdrawing—and on and on it goes when we do not see the worlds of others.

7. And if there had been any hope of creating partnership with one another, those hopes are diminished if not evaporated.

Reflection: *As you know yourself, when stuff happens that is noxious or a mystery, about how long does it take you to run through the above list? [Hint: Some readers measure their reaction time in nanoseconds.]*

Scene 2
From Spatial Blindness to Spatial Sight

What if, instead of making up stories,

we could know the real story?

What if, instead of seeing only the local picture,

we were able to see the whole picture?

What if, instead of reacting to stuff,

we could see the context behind that stuff?

This is the possibility of spatial sight.

6 Seeing Context

In organizations, much of the time
we think we are dealing person-to-person
when in fact we are dealing context-to-context.

Tops Surviving in a World of Complexity and Accountability

When interacting with *Tops*,
we are not just dealing person to person;
we are dealing with people living—sometimes struggling to
survive—in a world of **complexity** and **accountability**—
lots of issues to deal with,
difficult issues,
unpredictable issues,
issues they thought were taken care of that keep coming
back,
as well as issues regarding the direction, culture, growth, and
structure of the system.
And Tops are accountable for the successes and failures of the
system.

If we are able to see into Top's world, we may have a better sense of what happened to our memo to the top executive suggesting improvements in the operation—why we got no response. It may be that Top experienced our well-intentioned suggestion as just one more complication in an already overcomplicated life. It's also possible that Top, feeling responsible for the overall operation, experienced our cavalierly offered suggestion as a criticism.

It may also be that if we see Top's world more clearly, we can come up with smarter strategies for getting our proposals heard. Can we come across in a way that is seen as reducing the complexity of Top's world rather than increasing it? Can we come across in a way that communicates that we share responsibility for the system?

Bottoms Surviving in a World of Invisibility and Vulnerability

When interacting with *Bottoms*,
we are not just dealing person to person,
we are dealing with people living—sometimes struggling to
survive—in a world of **invisibility** and **vulnerability**.
They often are not seen by higher-ups,
and higher-ups can influence their lives in major and minor
ways:

- They change pension and health-care plans
- They reorganize
- They shut down plants

- They come up with new initiatives
- They acquire new entities
- They divest themselves of others

And all of this happens *to* Bottoms.

If we are able to see into Bottom's world, we may have a better idea of why our workers greeted our initiative with a wall of resistance. Given that higher-ups are always doing things *to* them, it's easy to see how our initiative was experienced as just another case of "Them doing it to us again." And if we see into Bottom's world more clearly, it may be that we can come up with better strategies for gaining involvement. How can we acknowledge their experience of vulnerability? And how can we position our initiative such that it reduces rather than increases that vulnerability?

Middles Surviving in a Tearing World

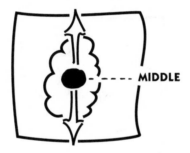

When interacting with *Middles*,
we are not just dealing person to person;
we are dealing with someone living in—sometimes struggling
to survive in—a **tearing** world.
They are pulled between you and others.
What you want from them, they don't have;
they need to go to others to get it.
And what others want from them,
they need to come to you to get.

They experience "simple" requests *from* you or others
as complex tearing *between* you and others.

If we are able to see into Middle's world, we have a better understanding of why our supervisor's response was so weak and wishy-washy. Because Middle doesn't have what we asked for, and because Middle would have to go to someone else to get it, it's crystal clear to us that our "simple" request is not so simple in that Middle world. It's easy to see how our request creates *more tearing* on Middle.

And if we are able to see into Middle's world, we might come up with more effective strategies for working with Middle to get what we need. How can we acknowledge the tearing on Middle, rather than poking fun at it or making it worse? How can we support Middle in getting what we need? How can we reduce the tearing rather than increase it?

Customers Surviving in a World of Neglect

When interacting with *Customers*,
we are not just dealing person to person;
we are dealing with people living in—and sometimes
struggling to survive in—a world of **neglect**.

They are not getting the attention they feel they deserve;
they are shunted from one person to another;
products and services are not coming to them as fast as they
want, at the level of quality they want, and at a satisfactory
price.
["PLOP" is the sound of product or service not quite making
it to you.]

And if we are able to see into Customer's world, we have a better understanding of why our Customer reacted to our nice gesture with anger and sarcasm. Customer was not interested in a tour of the facility. Customer was not interested in coffee and donuts. Customer was not interested in completing our customer satisfaction questionnaire. Customer was only interested in quality service, and quality service was not forthcoming. It's easy to see how Customer experienced all of our nice gestures as *more neglect.*

And if we are able to see our Customer's situation, we may be better able to develop the relationship both we and Customer want. How do we decrease Customer's experience of neglect rather than increase it?

■　■　■

In the story to follow, we can see how the same configuration of events can be experienced differently depending on one's systemic "world."

7 The "Truth" About Jack

An old proverb says: "We see people not as they are but as we are." To which we add: "And who we are is shaped by the systemic context in which we exist."

Jack is fired.

Jack's manager says,
"Jack was a pain in the butt, always complaining. The reorganization worked out perfectly. We no longer had any need for him. When I learned he was causing trouble for his group, that was the perfect opportunity to let him go. I asked the Tops if I could fire him, and they said go ahead."

One of Jack's coworkers says,
"I liked Jack. We were a tight group. I never saw him do anything wrong, nothing that would warrant firing. When I learned he was fired, I was scared: If they could fire him for whatever he did, then I wasn't safe either."

Jack's manager says,
"I was under pressure from the Tops. They were looking to me for production. There were Customers to satisfy, contracts to be signed, work to be done. The other group members were ready to work, but not Jack. Whenever I came to the group with work to be done, Jack always had these issues he needed to talk about. I just couldn't get the work done with him around."

A Customer says,
"When I learned that Jack was fired, I hired him immediately. I needed some creative help on my project and wasn't getting it. I never experienced Jack as a troublemaker. While working for me, he was a dedicated, hard-working, creative employee. As for the firing, all Jack ever wanted was respect. What was wrong with that?"

Jack says,
"In the beginning, the Manager asked us to come up with some creative ideas on a project. We put a lot of energy into that, and then we

learned that the decision had been made and the Customer hadn't even heard our ideas. Then the Manager tells us we've been put on a new project. We start on that project, only to learn there's a reorganization and our group is being broken up. It's crazy, and I'm frustrated. I want us all to talk about what's been happening to us. But the Manager says there's no time for that; there's work to be done, and the reorganization to be implemented. Finally, I'm given a new job: I'm going to do the design work for all the groups. I like that; it seems like a good assignment; I'm ready to go. Then I look around and see that all the groups are doing their own design work! I'm bewildered and totally frustrated. The next thing I know, I'm fired."

A second member of Jack's group says (sheepishly),

"I made a mistake. I was in the men's room and I made a casual comment to the Manager about Jack being a problem. It was a joke, nothing serious. Jack wasn't any big problem for us, but you could see that he was aggravating the Manager. I made a joke about it—something to say in the men's room. I never dreamt it would lead to this."

Jack's Manager says,
"That was all I needed."

A Top says to Jack's Manager,
"You think firing Jack was your idea? The Tops had already made the decision to fire him. Here we were running around like crazy trying to keep this organization afloat. Every time I pass this guy in the hall—I mean every time—he's got some complaint: his equipment, the temperature, his work assignment, the Manager. Every time I pass him, it's another complaint. When you came into the office, we had already made the decision to fire him."

So what is the truth about Jack?

Is he a troublemaker? Or is he a regular group member not much different from the rest? Is he a whining complainer the organization would best be rid of? Or is he an innocent, frustrated victim of management ineptitude? And what about that dedicated, hard-working, creative employee the Customer saw? Is that the real Jack?

The truth about Jack? Well, it depends as much on the conditions of your world as it does on who he is.

- In the world of a harried Top overwhelmed by complexity and accountability, the truth is that Jack is an unnecessary complication.
- In the world of a Middle torn between pressures from above and below, the truth is that Jack's "simple request for conversation" is more unwelcome tearing.
- In the world of Jack's associate group members who share his condition of invisibility and vulnerability, the truth is that Jack is an OK guy not much different from the rest.
- In the world of a Customer starved for service, the truth is that Jack is the answer to his prayers.

Jack was fired. To what effect? Again, it depends on where you stand.

The firing simplified the life of Tops,

it reduced the tearing of Middles,

it heightened the vulnerability of Bottoms,

and it resulted in much-needed service for the Customer.

But doesn't this tell us more about the others' worlds than it

does about Jack?

8 Charlotte Is a Problem

What difference would it make if we could see "stuff" from a systemic lens rather than a personal one?

Charlotte hates her job. She sees the company president as distant, arrogant, and uncaring. Charlotte's supervisor sees Charlotte as surly and uncooperative; "not a team player" is how he described it in her performance evaluation.

It wasn't always this way. Let's see where this problem started.

Some months ago, something was bothering Charlotte, something about the workflow that had been causing redundancy, misallocation of resources, costly errors, and diminished productivity. On her own, she did a careful study of the situation and, convinced that she was onto something, she spent her evenings writing a detailed report that included her observations, the apparent costs to the system, evidence of mismanagement (she was a bit caustic here), and her vision of how the workflow should be structured, along with the steps she felt would turn things around and ensure success. In the end, this was a detailed report, meticulously done, twenty-five single-spaced pages, with charts and graphs. Charlotte was proud of her work and the fact that she did this at her own initiative and on her own time, and she was truly excited about making a positive contribution to the organization.

Charlotte finished her report and sent it off to the company president. Then she waited. And she waited. Certainly there would be a phone call, a meeting, some acknowledgment of her contribution, maybe a bonus; even a promotion wouldn't have been out of the question. Something. But nothing came.

A week went by. Two weeks. Still nothing. Hope waned, and bitterness began to settle in. *Those executives*, she thought; *they go off to these programs on partnership or leadership or empowerment; they learn all the right words, but in the end it doesn't mean anything. It's more of the same old arrogance of top management. They really don't care.*

That marked the end of Charlotte as a highly motivated worker. Now she's angry; she has her evaluations (all negative) of the president; she is feeling righteous—*I did the right thing and what did it get me?* She's lost interest in pursuing her productivity project, and she is not averse to sharing her feelings with her coworkers.

■　■　■

Not to let the president off the hook, but Charlotte did have a choice: to play in the Side Show or the Center Ring.

"Stuff" happens;

you can take it personally

or treat it systemically;

one takes you to the Side Show,

the other to the Center Ring.

9   Center Ring or Side Show?

Organizational life (all of life) is a circus
with stuff coming at us from many directions—
noxious stuff,

mysterious stuff,

minus stuff.

In the circus of life we have two choices:
We can head for the Side Show
or stay in the Center Ring .
In the Side Show
we take the actions of others personally.
This brings us:

- Lots of drama, attractive stories with good parts for *us*—we are either the hero of our story or the poor, blameless victim of those bad guys
- Plenty of excuses why we don't have to do anything
- Plenty of righteous indignation

It also results in:

- Wasted, misdirected energy
- Loss of potential partnerships
- Diminished contributions to the system

Or

we can head for the Center Ring
where we take others' worlds into account.
What are *they* dealing with?
In the Center Ring:

- We have more understanding of others' worlds, more empathy with them.

- We may be less quick to judge others, to see them as malicious, insensitive, incompetent.
- We don't get hooked by the stuff; we don't let it stop us.
- We stay focused on what it is we are trying to make happen.
- We are strategic; we take others' worlds into account.
- We ease the condition of others to make it possible for them to do what we need them to do.
- We work to create or remain in productive partnerships with others.

Questions to think about:

1. Why do we spend so much time in the Side Show?

2. What are the system consequences of the Side Show?

Reflection: *Just think about some situation, present or past, in which you are or have been in the Side Show. You have fallen out of partnership with another person. You have your story that explains the situation. There's a lot of emotion wrapped up in that story. Your role is clear; you are the blameless one (hero or victim). Now ask yourself: what would you have to give up or let go of to move from the Side Show to the Center Ring?*

Seeing systems is not simply a minor shift in behavior. The Side Show is simple, reflexive: We're OK, and there's no further action we need to take. The Center Ring challenges us: Can we let go of our story? Can we let go of our evaluation of the Other? Can we let go of our righteousness? Can we stay in the process rather than ending it? Can we be strategic rather than reactive? When we choose the Center Ring, we choose a different order of *being* for ourselves.

The Side Show is predictable, but it is not inevitable.

The Center Ring is not predictable, but it is a human

possibility.

10 Times Out of Time: Seeing the Whole

How can we see the big picture in our day-to-day system life within the context of our family, our work group, our organization? It may be that life needs to imitate art. Let me share with you a dilemma I experienced in the early days of the Organization Workshop. We would set up the organization—with Tops, Middles, Bottoms, and Customers—and turn it loose. Action would break out all over the place—interactions within groups and across groups. I would run anxiously from place to place with my yellow pad, trying to track the action. After all, I was the one who set up this exercise (the Top), so it was important that I understand what was happening in order to help others learn from it.

It was impossible. I couldn't keep up with the action; too much was happening in too many different locations. And even if I could see it all—which I couldn't—there was important information that was invisible to me. *I had no access to people's experiences*—what were they thinking and feeling? How were they experiencing their worlds? How were they experiencing people in other parts of the system? Eventually we solved the problem by creating the Time Out of Time (TOOT). And having created it, it became clear that *it was less important that I saw what was happening throughout the system than that all system members saw it*. So let's see how the TOOT works.

"Stuff" Happens!

The exercise begins . . . and "stuff" happens everywhere. Tops are feeling overwhelmed: Customers looking to them for service; Middles looking for information and direction; basic issues about the organization that need to be decided. Middles are pressed by their Bottoms for information and direction that Middles don't have. Bottoms aren't getting the direction or feedback or the big picture. Customers aren't getting the attention they need. Work on projects gets started, is taken away, and disappears into a black hole. The organization appears to be disjointed (Middles can't get their act together, there are inconsistencies in reward systems). Some projects are drawing lots of attention, others are getting little or none. Tops are invisible to Bottoms, who wonder what, if anything, Tops do. Reorganizations happen, and many wonder

Why? Bottoms are wondering *What, if anything, is the added value of Middles?* Tops are deluged by demands coming from every direction; Bottoms get bonuses they feel they don't deserve, or they don't get bonuses they feel they *do* deserve. It's another day in the whitewater. Emotions run the full gamut—from excitement and challenge to anger, despair, hopelessness, apathy. And then it's time to TOOT.

We stop the organization, bring all the players into one place, and ask them to describe for one another what life is like in their part of the system: *Describe your world for us. What are the issues you are dealing with? What are you feeling? How are you seeing other parts of the system? Are they helping you or hindering you?*

First we hear from the Tops, then the Bottoms, then the Middles, and finally the Customers. Each part of the system begins to elucidate its world for the benefit of the others. Together they begin to illuminate the whole.

The TOOTs are an impactful part of the workshop. They are clearly the antidotes to spatial blindness. It is as if someone has turned on the lights for the entire system. Myths about others begin to shatter. The worker who was so evaluative of the Middle gains a better appreciation of the dilemmas Middle lives with; Tops hear firsthand about the frustrations of Bottoms; everyone hears the frustrations of Customers; the processes within groups are illuminated—the turf issues developing among the Tops, the inability of Middles to get together, the *we* versus *them* mentality developing among the Bottoms.

We set two basic guidelines for the TOOTs. *Tell the truth* (paint a picture for us; you are our experts on your part of the system; there is no other way for us to know what your world is like) and *listen carefully to others* (don't argue or debate, just let it in).

The TOOT's success depends on these two conditions:

- Are people willing and able to tell the truth of their experiences? In highly political systems in which people are committed to keeping secrets from one another, TOOTs will not work. Likewise, the quality of TOOTs suffers when people are unable to get in touch with or share their experiences.

- Are people willing and able to let in and accept as valid the experiences of others? The value of the TOOT will be diminished if people are committed to maintaining their stereotypes of others even in the face of disconfirming evidence.

When those two conditions are met, the results can be astounding. Some outcomes:

1. **Illumination.** People are intrinsically interested in moving beyond their narrow perspective to see "the big picture" and their part in it.

2. **Empathy.** People begin to have more empathy, understanding, and patience with one another. They are less quick to judge and slip into the Side Show.

3. **Depersonalization.** As people begin to see the contexts of others' actions—the issues they are dealing with—they are less apt to take these actions personally. They realize: *This is not an act directed against me.*

4. **Revitalization.** Instead of reacting to others—getting mad at them, getting even with them, withdrawing—people are more apt to stay in the Center Ring and put more of their energy into the work of the system.

5. **Problem solving.** Although it is *not* the purpose of the TOOT to solve problems, problems *are* identified—Tops are not getting the information they need, Customers are dissatisfied, efforts are being duplicated—and often, following the TOOT, these problems are addressed and dealt with *from any place in the system, not just by Tops.*

6. **Strategic planning.** As people begin to understand others' worlds, they see how their own actions have made it difficult for others to cooperate with them, and they see how they might get what they need by *easing* rather than exacerbating the conditions of others.

The organizational transformation following a TOOT is usually remarkable—more cooperation, less finger-pointing, more energy directed to the business of the system—and it all happens not through problem-solving but by simply illuminating one another's worlds.

There is another factor at play here. Following the TOOT, there is a brief, prepared (on newsprint or PowerPoint) conceptual input describing the worlds of Tops, Middles, Bottoms, and Customers pretty much as it has been described earlier in this section. This presentation maps closely the experiences people just had in the TOOT. This raises questions: *How is that possible? The presentation was prepared ahead of time, yet it described what we just went through.* In the midst of the action, what may have felt personal and specific to our situation couldn't have been personal or specific. If it were, how did *our* unique experiences get on that presentation? In such moments, there is the potential for a fundamental breakthrough: what happened to us was not personal and not specific; it can only be understood and managed systemically.

The TOOT Challenge

TOOTs are a possibility within most systems—the family, the work group, the plant, the business unit. Even when we work side by side with others, we are often blind to their experiences. We see the externals but not the internals; we see others' actions but not their thoughts and feelings.

The TOOT is a simple and powerful way to see the systems of which we are a part. All that is required is that we come together, share our experiences, and listen to the experiences of others.

What I appreciate most about the TOOT is that it is not prescriptive—you do not tell people what they should or should not do. I believe that people react positively to *not* being told what to do. The TOOT illuminates the system and, in that clarity, people see new choices. And the choices are theirs to make. Once we see clearly, most of us will do the right thing.

Our situation changes from one of blind reflex to enlightened choice.

TOOT Guidelines

1. EVERYONE SHOWS UP. It is important that all relevant parties be at the TOOT. Whether you are satisfied or dissatisfied, ready for new challenges or ready to quit, your experience is relevant to the TOOT. Come and be prepared to share your experience.

2. NO BUSINESS. The TOOT is not a staff meeting; it is not a time to solve problems (although what comes out at the TOOT often leads to subsequent problem solving). The purpose of the TOOT is to illuminate the system for all, so everyone can be clearer about the whole: What issues are people facing throughout the system?

3. TELL THE TRUTH. You are the expert on your part of the system. The rest of us are dependent on you to let us know what life is like for you: What is your world? What issues are you dealing with? What are your feelings?

4. LISTEN CAREFULLY TO OTHERS. Be open to the experiences of others. Discover their worlds, their feelings, the issues they are facing.

11 The TOOT Dilemma

The TOOT is like turning a light on in a dark room
when you thought the light was *already* on.

The TOOT confronts us with a dilemma:
We can listen to these others,
try to understand their worlds,
empathize with them,
work with them,
see them as OK people—
like us—
take their worlds into account,
try to ease their condition
just as we would like them to ease ours.

Or

we can stick with our story.

Our story may be more appealing than the TOOT story,

more dramatic,

bad guys (them),

good guys (us),

the blamed

and the blameless.

This is the tension the TOOT creates:

Our story

against Its story,

judgment

against empathy,

blame

against understanding,

reaction

against thought,

"Them"

against "all of us,"

good guys and bad guys

against just plain folks.

This is the tension of seeing systems.

You want to see your system?

Try TOOTs.

The challenge is this:

Are you willing to tell the truth?

Are you willing to listen to others?

Are you willing to give up *your* story

for Its story?

Scene 3
From Temporal Blindness to Temporal Sight

 **S** **patial blindness**

is about

seeing the part

without the whole.

Temporal blindness

is about

seeing the present

without the past.

12 The Invisible Histories of the Swims We Are In

Several years ago, Karen Oshry, Joe Meier, and I set about what we thought would be a simple task. We were going to assemble a photo history of one of our Power Labs: twenty or so snapshots of events along with brief commentaries. *Three years later we completed the project!* (In fairness to us, not all of our time was spent on this project, but we spent considerably more time on it than we had anticipated.) Our plan at the outset was simple: Identify certain key events, match up the pictures, provide a few illuminating descriptions, and that would be that. Unfortunately, there are no isolated events in systems. *Everything connects with everything else.* We would identify a particular interaction and then get curious about what had led to it and what had followed from it. Each discovery led us to other questions and other discoveries. In the end, there was a story, a three-hundred-page history, a clear and coherent picture of the life of this social system.[3]

From our outside perspective, this was a beautiful story—beautiful in that it had form, direction, movement, and clearly evolving patterns of interaction within and across the classes. This was not a set of random events, it was a story that was going someplace; yet in the living of that history, no system member had experienced its beauty. For them, life was pretty much as we experience it daily—a collection of random events or loosely connected events and ups and downs, rather than a richly textured unfolding story in which we play a part.

From this and many other experiences that followed the compilation of the photo history, I am led to the hypothesis that *in all systems there is a story that unfolds*—a history that has shape, movement, pattern, and direction. Each of our families has a coherent history—an unfolding tale about how each of us got to this point in time. Each of us is in touch with various pieces of our history, but the histories of our families as wholes tend to be invisible to us. This is true for our work teams, our circles of friends, our task forces and organizations, and all the social systems of which we are a part. The histories of the "swims" we are in are invisible to us. Yet those histories are keys to our experiences of the swim.

The question in terms of seeing systems is this: Can we see our system stories? And if so, what difference can that "seeing" make?

What follows are pieces of three stories:

"History's Burst of Illumination" demonstrates the power that unraveling the histories of our systems has in fundamentally altering our experience of the present.

"Bart and Barb: A System Evolves . . . Perfectly" communicates in encapsulated form what I mean by a beautiful story: No one sets out to create a story, yet a story emerges. The dramatic form of the story is as follows: Two members of the Elite struggle over the direction the society will take. First one member becomes dominant while the other is suppressed, then the second becomes dominant while the first is suppressed. Then the society splits and two distinctly different societies emerge, one for each Elite. The original society disappears; members dissatisfied with one society find a more suitable place for themselves in the other. In the end there is a total transformation of the original society.

This is a history with a direction, an unfolding. Neither Bart nor Barb nor any of the other members of this system experience its beauty, form, shape, or coherence. They all have their good and bad moments, their joys and frustrations, their attractions to one another, and their hostilities. But the story of the whole is invisible to them.

"Bart and Barb" makes us wonder about our own systems: What are their stories? And if we could see those stories, how would that deepen our experience of our systems?

In "'Anthropology' or Mick Gets Wiped Out," we see the cost of temporal blindness: A Middle breaks down and drops out of society. The causes of this breakdown are invisible to all until the history is revealed, and then they are crystal clear. Anthropology reveals some of the history of this incident; it also gives us a glimpse into the processes used in the Power Lab to weave together a system's history. This piece raises a dilemma for us. We see the powerful impact our systems' histories can have; we see the potential that lies in revealing our histories; and we see what an immense challenge we face in doing so.

Anthropology, as described here, is probably not the most effective technology for helping members fully experience the rich flow and interconnectedness of their system lives. Our work suggests that members need to be more directly involved in unraveling their own history (see **50**, "Immigrant Martha Has a Breakdown"). The Anthropologist's central function may be to help in identifying key events and interactions along the way and in providing processes whereby system members can keep ongoing records of their experiences. "Applied Anthropology: Unraveling System History," the last item in this section, offers some guidelines for the process.

13 History's Burst of Illumination

In the earliest versions of the Organization Workshop, there were no TOOTs and no intervening conceptual inputs. As a consequence, events generally spiraled downward from bad to worse, Side Shows leading to ever more dramatic Side Shows; and when the exercises ended there would be considerable misunderstanding and ill will, requiring hours of review and analysis. In one workshop we were pressed for time; we needed to cut down the time for both the exercise and the review. What began as a practical exercise in time management ended up yielding a startling result. The arrangement we settled on was as follows:

The exercise was to run for seven "days." Each day would be only five minutes long.

Following each day, there would be a two-minute period in which participants made diary entries. *What happened during the day?*

And so it went for seven "days": five minutes of action followed by two minutes of reflection.

At the end of the seventh day, people reported what their experiences were at the end of the exercise. The reports were full of the usual recriminations, ill will, and finger pointing, along with heavy doses of righteousness.

Then we began a sequential debriefing, a process we had never before used.

The sequence was as follows:

We went back to the beginning.

Everyone took a few moments to review the day one reflections, then there was a five-minute period in which we heard from all parts of the system. So we had a fairly clear picture of what had happened during day one: what was happening with the Tops, Middles, Bottoms, and Customers.

We followed that procedure for each day: a few moments to review the diary entries, then a report from each part of the system.

And so it went for the seven days.

As the sharing progressed, we all could see the various stories unfolding from each part of the system and how these stories were intersecting with one another. We had a helicopter view; from this vantage point we could see two or more cars coming from different directions racing toward a collision.

As the final report came out, it was crystal clear to all of us how we came to this ending: how all the misunderstandings developed, how the collisions occurred. There was momentary silence, then a remarkable thing happened: we broke out in spontaneous applause. It was a gleeful moment. Much laughter and shaking of heads in disbelief. All the recriminations gone, all the ill feelings, the righteousness. All gone. Nothing remained but pure clarity. We had what was, for me, the rarest of experiences. We saw our history, and that seeing fundamentally transformed our experience of the present. We will see such a moment again in **50**, "Immigrant Martha Has a Breakdown."

This process of sequentially debriefing the history of events *by all parties* remains a discovery whose full potential is yet to be tapped.

14 Bart and Barb: A System Evolves . . . Perfectly

A Power Lab Tale of The Traditionalist and the Humanist

Bart and Barb are the central players in the Elite,
cocaptains of the ship,
battling with one another over the course the ship should
take.

Louis and Minnie—
other members of the Elite—
are ballast in the hold,
shifting from side to side,
sometimes toward Bart,
sometimes toward Barb.

Bart is Traditionalist,
striving to maintain the system as he found it:
a harsh system,
a system of Haves and Have-Nots.
All power rests with the Elite—
the Robe of Justice,
the Food,
the Housing,
Work, Information, Culture—
all controlled by the Elite.

Barb is Humanitarian,
a seer of new possibilities.
"We are the Elite," she says.

"We are not stuck with the past;
we can create a new world.
No need to be harsh.
We can take care of people,
make decisions *with* them,
share our power *with* them."

Bart fears Barb.
"We'll have to watch you closely," he says.
"You're dangerous.
You'll turn our world upside down.
Chaos."

Barb feels controlled by Bart.
"Lighten up," she says.
"Give," she says.
"Why not give?
What harm will it do?"

"Chaos," says Bart.
"Chaos might not be so bad," says Barb.

The ballast slides toward Bart.
Louis and Minnie agree:
Barb is a danger,
she must be controlled.
A rule is created:
An Elite can be ejected from the Elite
by the vote of three other Elites.
(Watch out for rules that control others;
they may come back for you.)

The ship heads out along Bart's course—
Tradition—
the way it is, is the way it was.
Barb is captive on her own ship,
a reluctant Elite,
confused,
depressed,
beaten,
purposeless.

Barb Fights Back

Barb fights back from depression and defeat;
she struggles to change the system from within;
she struggles against Bart;
she is the voice of reason,
flexibility,
change,
hope—
a message of considerable appeal
to some Have-Nots.

The ballast shifts toward Barb.
Louis and Minnie
support Barb's liberalizing efforts
while undermining Bart
and his Robes
and his Court
and his calls for Tradition.
The ship shifts course,

heading out along Barb's course.
Now Bart is captive on the ship;
his Robes are laughed at,
his pronouncements ignored.

He fights for Tradition;
he is scoffed at,
publicly disowned by the Elite.
His rule is used against him;
he is voted out of the Elite.

Bart is confused,
depressed,
beaten,
purposeless.

Bart Fights Back

Bart fights back from depression and defeat.
He separates from Barb and Louis and Minnie;
he takes a piece of Elite property for himself;
he establishes a new society.
So now there are two societies—
and they are such different societies.
Take your choice:
It's Barb's
or Bart's.

The Hill and the Slum

Barb's society is the Hill—
uptown,
the big house,
overlooking the ocean,
food, money,
seriousness,
a yearning for higher purpose.

Bart's society is the Slum—
downtown,
dark and messy,
smoky, very smoky,
wine and beer,
playfulness,
and aimlessness.

Barb's leadership is purposeful;
Bart's is formless,
wandering,
chaotic (one might say).

Barb's society seeks higher meaning—
some cause "out there"
that we can serve.

Bart's society is primal:
How do we get more beer and wine
and cigarettes?
An all-night dance hall?
Games to play?

Barb's society
moves out to find a cause.
Bart's society
moves out to hustle cigarettes
and cash in empties.
Barb's society attracts one disgruntled Immigrant,
who, with Barb, finds meaning.
Bart's society attracts one overworked Middle,
who, with Bart, finds freedom.

The Middles "dis-integrate" perfectly:
one joins Barb;
one joins Bart;
one joins neither.

The Society Blossoms

The society has blossomed
like a flower—
beautifully,
symmetrically,
miraculously.
Everyone has found a place.
What could be more perfect?

That's how it looks from the outside.
And from the inside?

Bart and Barb cross paths on the street:
Barb looking for supplies;
Bart looking for fun.
"Barb!" Bart cries happily.
Barb looks away.
"Wanna play Pictionary?!" cries Bart excitedly.
"F—- off!" shouts Barb
purposefully.

■   ■   ■

An alternate ending to this tale would have all members in both societies standing in a circle, glasses raised on high, celebrating their remarkable collective achievement. There was no master hand behind this, yet the system evolved from one that worked for few to one that worked for most if not all. They would have cheered one another—Bart and Barb and all the others—for having had the courage to push up against one another, to leave spaces that had enmeshed them, to seek and create spaces that liberated them. All of this would have been possible had they been able to recreate their history.

What difference would it make

if we could see the unfolding stories

of our various system lives—

the family,

the organization,

the community,

our circle of friends—

if we could see

how we and others

got to this point in time?

What difference would it make

if we could see the day-to-day events of life

not as isolated events

but as pieces of a rich tale

with form,

and pattern,

and direction?

15 "Anthropology" or Mick Gets Wiped Out

A cautionary tale for any Middle who has been crushed by invisible behind-the-scenes forces

■

CENTRAL CHARACTERS

Elites: Eddy, Edgar, Evelyn

Middles: Mick, Moira

Immigrants: Betty, Bob

Anthropologists: Barry, Gisela, Jonathan

Part I. Wipeout

Mick was a Middle in one of our Power Labs. After two days on the job, he quit. He quit the society and he quit the program. Mick left in a fury. He would not talk nor listen to anyone. He simply walked off.

A day later we heard from Mick. He was still in the area, emotionally unsteady ("I can't go home in this shape").

Let me assure the concerned reader that Mick returned to the program, and at program's end he was completely healed, in high spirits, and delightfully enlightened regarding the travails of Middles in organizations. What troubles me is that the special conditions of the Power Lab made this healing and enlightenment possible, and these same conditions do not exist for the hordes of Middles in organizations who are being "wiped out" daily.

Let's look at the events that led up to Mick's breakdown. As a Middle in the Power Lab, Mick functioned between the Elite, who owned and controlled most of the society's resources and institutions, and the Immigrants, who entered the society with little more than the clothes on their backs.

Much of Mick's time was spent navigating between pressures from the impoverished Immigrants to change the system and those from the Elite to maintain it. Mick's job was complex; he was living in a downsized system that required him to wear several hats. He was responsible for the Employment Center: lining up full- and part-time jobs for the Immigrant laborers, scheduling work, and serving as Paymaster. He was also the Work Supervisor and the society's Police Chief. The work/police combination regularly put him at odds with himself. ("As Police Chief I'm inclined to enforce the law; however, doing so can have negative consequences for my Workers' morale.")

Mick had been a diligent Middle—never shirking his many and complex duties. And he was scrupulously evenhanded. When dealing with the Immigrants, he upheld the Elite's rules and standards. ("No, I don't believe you are entitled to a bed or a meal without paying for it.") And when dealing with the Elite, he consistently carried forth concern for the Immigrants' position. ("All they want is to be heard by you.")

Mick was crunched in the middle. He was angry at the Immigrants. ("Sometimes I feel the same way with my kids. If they dropped off the face of the earth, I wouldn't care. You give and you give and you give, and it becomes an entitlement. Even when the Immigrants say they want to help us, it's really that they want something from us.") And he felt consistently undermined by the Elite. ("We have people who break the rules, and you Elite don't do anything about it. As Police Chief I have things to enforce, but there's no backup from you. It's a joke. The Immigrants say, 'If we hold out long enough, the Elite will give in.'")

Now to the triggering event: The Elite came to Mick with a proposition. They had a piece of property they were willing to make available to the Immigrants. This was a major move. The new house was to serve two purposes: to relieve overcrowding and to provide space for a new societal institution.

Mick was concerned that the house was going to be seen by the Immigrants as another victory. ("They bark, we jump; they bark, we jump.") He wanted the Elite's agreement that *he* would manage the process, that it would not be tossed in by the Elite over the Middles' heads. Mick said to the Elite: "What's even more important to the Immigrants than the house is that they have a say."

The conversation with the Elite went on for close to an hour. The Elite proposed that Bob (an Immigrant) jointly manage the process with Mick.

"No," said Mick. "Bob reports to me. It would undermine me. I need to manage the process." And so it was agreed. *The house would be*

*put into play; Mick was to manage the process; the Elite would not under-
mine him.*

Twenty minutes later Mick was meeting with the Immigrants. He
told them about this new piece of property that was about to become
available. He told them that the Elite were hoping this would have an
uplifting effect on the community. He told them that it was up to them
to decide how to use the house, how to manage the process. Mick
believed he was coming in with a big piece of news until he was interrupted in midsentence by Immigrant Bob.

"I want you to know," says Bob, "that the Elite have agreed to
meet with Betty and me on that very same subject in fifteen minutes."

Mick gulped. He was clearly shaken. He gamely went on with the
rest of his agenda, but he had just been wiped out. The next morning
he quit the society and the lab.

Part II. A Simple Explanation

This appears to be a straightforward tale of betrayal. Mick has been
a hardworking Middle, laboring to adjust to the incompatible demands
of the Elite and the Immigrants. He has been under considerable pressure from both sides. He is angry at the Immigrants, and he feels
unsupported and undermined by the Elite. He finally manages to establish a solid set of agreements with the Elite, and within the hour those
agreements are broken. He is to bring the good news to the
Immigrants, *but they already have the news.* He alone is to manage the
process, *but now it appears to be in the hands of two of his employees.*
Mick's emotions are complex—his rage at both the Immigrants and the
Elite is beyond his usual coping range. At the same time, he blames
himself. ("I was given a simple task. If only I had done it right. I feel
like a failure.") And finally he feels that the Mick he knew has disap-
peared in this process. ("Where did I lose myself? I lost *me* in this
process.")

Part III. "Anthropology"

Things are not as they seem. There is quite a different story to be
told here, a startling story. Everything that I described did happen just

as I described it, yet it all adds up to one small piece of the truth. For example: What if I told you that there was no betrayal here? Would you believe me?

First, let me tell you how we know what we know. I've already made some references to the role of the Anthropologist at the Power Lab. We have a team of them whose job is to keep the history of the society as it unfolds. It is a grueling job—Anthros are usually the first to rise in the morning and the last to retire at night. They go around with heavy notebooks and a supply of pens. Their assignment is to be everywhere—to observe, to record conversations, to summarize events. One thing they are clearly told *not* to do is to interpret events or evaluate them. Simply witness. Observe. Interview. Write and write and write. Stay close to the facts. Don't jump too quickly to patterns. Don't even look for patterns. Stick to the data, and pray that the patterns will emerge.

Anthropology is possible at the Power Lab because of the contract Anthros make with participants: "We have access to everything. No meetings—no matter how private—are closed to Anthros." But because the Power Lab is by design a very political system, we promise confidentiality: "Information from one part of the system will not be passed on to people in other parts of the system. This information will only be used once the societal experience has ended." It is only through such a compact that we gain the access we need to gather the system's history.

It very quickly becomes clear why such a contract would be difficult to establish in most other systems. The commitment to be a true "learning organization" would have to be quite strong.

Consider, for example, a conversation I witnessed among human resources executives. A strike was impending at one plant. The human resources executive said, with a sheepish grin, "To tell the truth, we could take a strike. That would give us the opportunity to shut the plant down and move to the Midwest, closer to headquarters and cheaper labor." So, while the union worked on strategies for squeezing management, management waited, only too eager to be squeezed. This was information that management in that organization was not about to make available to a roving Anthropologist, knowing that eventually their strategy would be revealed.

This type of anthropology can be a powerful tool for deepening our understanding of social system life. It has great potential for illuminating life for system members—and for most systems, it would require an immense shift in thinking about transparency and secrecy.

And so the following story emerges *only* because three Anthropologists—Jonathan, Gisela, and myself—happened to be stationed at various locations, notebooks and pens in hand, as the tale unfolded.

Part IV. An Arm's-Length Elite

As the society was unfolding, we Anthros were struggling to develop a picture of the Elite: the form their interactions were taking, the issues they were dealing with collectively. It was frustrating. There were so little data. We looked for meetings of the Elite, but there were few such meetings, and at what meetings there were, very little business transpired. There were no momentous battles among the Elite (an infrequent pattern, as Elites with differing opinions as to how the system should develop typically battle with one another for control; see **39**, "Territorial Tops: Stuck on Differentiation"). So these Elites were not a closely knit team, nor were they enmeshed in turf battles. *Then it struck us how the absence of data was the data.* These were arm's-length Elite. Each had his or her area of responsibility, which each oversaw with relatively little interaction with the others. There were striking differences among the Elite in their personal styles and visions for the society. These differences were briefly confronted at the beginning of their life together, but not thereafter.

Two of the Elites, Eddie and Ernest, had sharply contrasting styles. Eddie valued energy—his own and others. He operated intuitively. He did not need complex, well-thought-out rationales for action. He was comfortable stirring things up. He had little need to please the Immigrants or to feel personally responsible for improving their conditions.

Ernest was much more rational in his thinking than Eddie was—even if things *felt* right, for him that was not sufficient evidence to prove that they *were* right. Ernest needed rationales and frameworks within which his and others' actions fit. Ernest and Eddie had strong negative feelings toward one another, feelings that were played out in action but not confronted head-on.

Evelyn, the third member of the Elite, stayed clear of the tension between Eddie and Ernest. She quietly went about her business—organizing the complex relationships with the dining room—good at details, arranging, cleaning up.

Periodically, an Anthropologist would capture a graphic image of this arm's-length Elite pattern—not yet realizing that it was a pattern. We would trudge up to the Elite house, hoping to find some interaction to capture. (What are you going to write in your notebook if no one is talking?) Instead of interaction, there would be Ernest in his car on his cell phone talking to his family; inside the house, Evelyn sitting in the living room or looking for Eddie; upstairs, Eddie reading in bed. When Evelyn finally went upstairs and found Eddie, she carried on a brief conversation with him—Evelyn in the doorway, Eddie lying in bed—at a distance of approximately fifteen feet.

In the Anthropologist's notebook, all of this made for fairly dull reading. Only later did its significance become clear.

Part V. The Anthropologists' Ordeal: Capturing the System's Story

Before unraveling the story of Mick's wipeout, we need to talk more about the unraveling process. We Anthropologists have a very specific assignment. Toward the end of each Power Lab, we are given a two- to three-hour time slot with a specific agenda: to help participants see the totality of the system of which they have been a part. Our assignment is to capture the system's story in some coherent fashion that illuminates the experiences of the individuals within it. We are given twenty-four hours to complete our task.

We closet ourselves. Among us we have over five hundred pages of handwritten notes: snatches of conversation—no interpretations, no evaluations, only who said what to whom. Many of our notes are barely legible or are illegible. They are hastily written. Sometimes there are too many people talking at once, or we have recorded conversations among people walking from one place to another (try writing while walking). There may have been conversations held in the rain or in the dark. We have no notes on apparently key events that happened when none of us was present. There were more discrete events than we had Anthropologists to cover them. There were times when we were so fatigued that we just stopped writing. We are overwhelmed by the size of the task and by our limitations.

At the outset, the process of piecing together the whole story is fascinating. It is a remarkable experience—a rare privilege—to stand outside a system with these relics and fossils of existence and bring to life a coherent whole. In time, reality strikes—then, panic! We are proceeding too slowly. A quarter of our preparation time is gone, and we have covered merely an eighth of the system's life. We need to speed it up. We briefly entertain certain illusions—we can skip certain parts; we can focus only on important events. We try; we fail. We are trapped in our own systemic thinking. We jump ahead only to find that in order to understand "ahead" we need to back up. Everything connects with everything else. There are no shortcuts. So we plow on.

We do not get to the immediate events surrounding Mick's wipeout until 2:00 A.M. Until then, we think we have a clear picture of what happened. Ernest and Evelyn had betrayed Mick. They promised him that he could manage the new house deal; they promised they would not undermine him; then they betrayed him. When we saw what had really happened, there was a collective gasp from the Anthropologists.

Part VI. When Agendas Collide

It is 2:00 A.M. The Anthropologists are reviewing their notes covering the evening events leading up to Mick's wipeout. The supposed big news of the early evening is the discrepancy in dinner menus. The Elite had chosen not to eat in the dining room (the usual arrangement); instead, they had their dinner—lobster with fixings accompanied by wine—delivered to their home. Meanwhile the Immigrants, only able to afford the Class B dinner, made do with franks and beans. Once again, however, the story is revealed not in the grand gesture but in the sideline and apparently less significant events. When all of these were pieced together, the following story unfolded.

The Elite were having their lobster dinner at their house. Gisela's sense was that nothing of importance happened at dinner. The conversation was subdued. As usual, there was little talk of business, and no decisions were made. The conversation took a lighthearted turn as the Elite began to play with fantasies of how they might use their as-yet unused piece of property: as a monastery for one of the more troublesome Immigrants; as a retreat house for women; as a center for the arts. [You, the reader, know the potential significance of this lighthearted conversation, because you know that the management of the new house became a central issue. But at the time and without foreknowledge, the discussion seemed unimportant, lighthearted dinner joviality—particularly because the subject was eventually simply dropped. It is possible that, were you the recording Anthropologist, the conversation might not even have made it into your notebook.]

Keep in mind: These are our arm's-length Elite.

Jonathan had been with the Immigrants at their franks and beans dinner. Here the conversation centered around whether the Immigrants could remain a unified group and, at the same time, allow and encourage individual members to pursue their own paths. Unbridled individuation became the theme. Some members were to work for change within the system, one was planning middle-of-the-night direct action against the Elite, and two (Bob and Betty) were setting out to explore entrepreneurial possibilities.

So now two stories began to unfold around our arm's-length Elite.

Jonathan tagged along with Bob and Betty as they sought out Eddie ("Are there any entrepreneurial opportunities in this community?"), while Barry came across Ernest and Evelyn talking about the possibilities of an Art House. [As the reader, you are now enjoying the global view; you probably have some good hunches as to how this scenario will unfold. As on-the-ground Anthropologists, however, we saw no pattern. Each of us was out there doing our job, writing it all down, not knowing whether the piece we were describing was worth the ink we were using.]

Immigrants Betty and Bob approached Elite Eddie, looking for entrepreneurial opportunities. Eddie dangled the possibility of the house in front of them. He talked about being willing to entertain serious proposals. "There is a window of opportunity," he said, "but it will close quickly."

Meanwhile, Barry stood by as Elites Evelyn and Ernest (at the usual arm's length from Eddie) were also thinking about the unused house. They formulated their own plan for bringing it into play, and an explicit part of their strategy was to involve the Middle Managers, Mick and Moira. Evelyn said, "I want to give them the resources they've been looking for."

And now two independent streams of events, which began at arm's length, hurtled toward collision.

Immigrants Bob and Betty went off to do some thinking about the new house, and they scheduled a follow-up meeting with Elite Eddie. At the same time, Elites Evelyn and Ernest brought their plan to Mick and Moira.

Mick worked out his agreements with Evelyn and Ernest (he'd manage the process; no undermining from the Elite). At the same time, Bob and Betty rejoined their group feeling some confidence that they could make a deal for the house.

Mick went to the Immigrants and made his "surprise" announcement, only to find out that Betty and Bob—his employees—were already working on their own deal.

Wipeout!

Part VII: More Pieces of the Puzzle

It's 2:30 A.M. We Anthropologists think we have this fairly well figured out, but there is still a puzzle. Why did Ernest and Evelyn allow this to happen? How could they have so easily violated the agreement they had made with Mick? We go back into our notebooks.

Gisela was at a late-night meeting involving Bob and Betty and all of the Elites. Ernest and Evelyn were there; they were watching Eddie complete his deal with Immigrants Betty and Bob. *Why didn't Ernest and Evelyn stop this?* Why didn't they talk about the agreement they had made with Mick just hours before?

Barry noted that when Immigrants Betty and Bob left the Immigrant meeting to meet with Elite Eddie, Middle Moira went with them. And Mick—still reeling from the shock of his "betrayal"—in a last gasp of Middle other-devotedness said to Moira, "Whatever you do, I want you to support them (Betty and Bob)."

Gisela noted that when all of the Elite met with Bob and Betty, Moira also was there, and she announced, "I am representing Mick."

"I am representing Mick." Puzzle piece added to piece added to piece until . . . another communal gasp escaped from the collective Anthropologist throat. Aha! There was no betrayal.

So here is the scene. It was a late-night meeting. The purpose was to conclude negotiations for the new house. Present were all of the

Elite: Eddie, Evelyn, and Ernest. Also present were two Immigrants: Bob and Betty. And there was Middle Moira. Middle Moira explained her presence at this meeting as representing Mick.

To Elite Eddie, this meeting was the culmination of his deal with Immigrants Betty and Bob.

To Elites Evelyn and Ernest, this was the culmination of their deal with Mick. To their way of thinking, *Moira was there representing Mick.* To their way of thinking, Mick must have made his presentation to the Immigrants, Bob and Betty had picked up on it, and this meeting was the natural outcome. Mick *was* managing the process, just as they had agreed he would.

So, according to everyone but Mick, there was no wipeout. When Mick left the program, it was just a case of personal instability. Case closed!

Part VIII. Without Anthropologists

If there had been no Anthropologists, what would the story have been?

Mick was wiped out.

He had a clear picture of how it happened. He was betrayed. His picture, however, was grossly inaccurate and incomplete. He was furious at the others, he was confused, and he focused much of the blame on himself. ("I was given a simple task and I failed.")

The Elites' absolutely central role in the wipeout was invisible to them. *Their arm's-length pattern was undoubtedly the single most powerful determinant in this scenario,* yet they were unlikely to see it. They had other explanations: too much stress, immaturity, or maybe the anti-social actions of certain Immigrants. (Remember the Immigrant who was planning some late-night harassment? Well, he did it. And he harassed the Middles' house as well as the Elites'. Could that be what drove Mick over the edge?)

Had there been no Anthropologists, there probably would be well-intentioned feedback to Mick (it's called Performance Management) about his managerial weaknesses and how to function more effectively. And Mick would likely take this feedback to heart. More attention to personal and professional development. That's the answer.

What Can We Do with This Knowledge?

There is some powerful knowledge here, but what can we do with it? We are blind to system history, and as a consequence we are at its mercy. This is one case of a wipeout that occurred because of system blindness. Because of our blindness, personal breakdowns happen; because of our blindness, we conjure up wrong explanations; because of our blindness, we propose misguided remedial actions.

In one respect, Mick's story is a rarity: we have been able to see the blindness. But do you have any doubt that similar wipeouts occur regularly and without Anthropologists to unravel the approximate truth? System blindness is everywhere. We know that. And the most dangerous thing about blindness is that when we're blind, we don't know we're blind. We think we see. We take what we see as the truth, and we act.

The question remains: Is it possible to see the system story and our part in it? And if so, what difference would that "seeing" make? If the Elite could have seen their arm's-length pattern and its effects on Mick and the rest of the system life, what other possibilities might that "seeing" have opened up for them? Had Mick been able to see the same, how might that have shifted his experience of himself? And what other strategies might that have opened up for him? It takes little imagination to recognize how such "seeing" might fundamentally reshape system life.

But how can such "seeing" happen? Can Anthropologists make it happen? Even in the learning environment of the Power Lab, Anthropologists walk a fine line. There is a sensitivity to their presence. Can they be trusted not to carry information from one part of the system to another? The more political the system, the more secrets there are to protect and the more sensitivity there is to "outsiders."

You might ask, couldn't Anthropologists put out clues without revealing specific data? For example, they could make this suggestion to the Elite: *You would do well to examine your pattern of interaction and the consequences it is having for the system.* That's possible. But how do we help Mick see the Elite pattern and its consequences for him? We might put out similar clues like fortune cookie messages: *Beware of arm's-length Elite.* For the Anthropologist, there is always the danger of pushing the wrong button, which then closes off access to the others.

It occurs to me that Anthropology *is* a possibility for our systems, and its presence would move systems to an entirely new level of existence. What if a system were committed to seeing itself? Anthropologists have access to all parts of the system. Their assignment is to see the system as it is—not to interpret it or evaluate it, but simply to capture its history, as it unfolds, as objectively as they can—and then, periodically, to feed the system's story back to system members. Could we live with that? Even when we have conflicting agendas?

In this story, *arms-length Elite* was the invisible pattern, invisible to all—Elite, Middles, and Immigrants—yet it was a pattern that had consequences for the whole system. Undoubtedly there are many such invisible patterns in many systems that have total system consequences. Anthropology, with its helicopter view of the whole, can make the invisible visible in ways that strengthen systems.

Let's go back to our human resources executive. The big secret is this: management might welcome a strike. That would give them the opportunity to shut down the plant and move closer to headquarters and a source of cheaper labor. What if that terrible secret were known? What if it were part of the system's open history? Would that destroy the system? Or would it change—greatly, I admit—the level of dialogue?

The ability to see the systems that we are a part of may be the next level of human evolution. Throughout our history, the absence of such "seeing" has resulted in endless cycles of misunderstanding, wrongful damage, abuse, oppression, and annihilation. Can we do better?

And could "Anthropology" be part of the solution?

16 Applied Anthropology: Unraveling System History

We have had but a handful of experiences in which a careful unraveling of a system's history has had a profound effect on system members. (See **50**, "Immigrant Martha Has a Breakdown" for a description of one such case.) To see such an incident, however, is to open oneself to a whole new possibility of system experience.

Because the experience is so rare, it is difficult to describe it. In essence, it is like moving from a flat plane of experience to a multidimensional one—like moving from seeing a drawing of a scene to entering into the scene itself.

We are just beginning to scratch the surface in our understanding of how to make such "seeing" possible. Here are some guidelines:

1. It helps if all system members keep journals of their experiences in the system—keeping track of dates and times of significant events and recording their reactions (thoughts and feelings) to these events.

2. It helps to have an Anthropologist or a team of Anthropologists (depending on the size of the system) to keep track of system events.

3. In the unraveling process, it helps to start in the present with a TOOT. What is the picture of the current system? How are people currently experiencing themselves, others, and the system? What are the issues and dilemmas they are facing now?

4. It helps to go back to the beginning: pick a point in time and gradually work your way forward to the present. At each point, have system members review their journals, get back in touch with their experiences at the time, and then share those experiences publicly.

5. In moving toward the present, stay alert to the story that's beginning to unfold—the pieces coming together from all parts of the system. When the process works, a bright shining light is cast on the present.

In this section we have examined two types of system blindness and two strategies for seeing systems.

The TOOT helps us to avoid spatial blindness: It allows us to see into the worlds of others in the system; to see others as they are, not as our myths and prejudices define them; to understand how our different worlds impact one another; and to illuminate more productive and satisfying ways of staying in partnership with one another while contributing to the health and effectiveness of our systems.

Anthropology helps us to avoid temporal blindness: It allows us to see our history—how we got to where we are—and to see the patterns and processes developing in the system that could be blocking and frustrating, and leading us to misunderstandings and unproductive conflict. Beyond that, seeing the whole of our story deepens and enriches our experience of life.

SEEING PATTERNS OF RELATIONSHIPS

Act II

In Act One we explored the consequences of our blindness to *external* factors—our inability to see other parts of our system and our system's history. In Act Two we will examine our *internal* blindness—our inability to see ourselves and the actions we take, without awareness or choice, that lead us out of the possibilities of partnership and into relationships of opposition, antagonism, disappointment, and warfare.

In Act Two we see human systems as constantly shifting patterns of relationship. Sometimes we are Top in a Top/Bottom relationship and sometimes we are Bottom in that relationship. Sometimes we are Middle between two or more Ends pulling at us and sometimes we are one of several Ends tugging at Middle. Sometimes we are Provider supplying services to a Customer and sometimes we are Customer.

For the most part, we humans do not see ourselves as being in *systemic relationships*. In our blindness to our relational blindness, we fall into familiar dances with one another—dances in which we become the Burdened Tops and Oppressed Bottoms, the Unsupported Ends and Torn Middles, the Judged Providers and the Righteously Done-to Customers.

The challenges are these: Can we see ourselves in *systemic relationship*? Can we recognize the dances *while we are dancing*? Can we, from whatever side of the relationship we are on, stop the unproductive and often destructive dances and, ultimately, transform them into dances that are more satisfying and more constructive?

Two New Characters

In Act Two our stage becomes a bit more crowded. We are joined by two new characters:

■

She: A scientist, a student of human systems, a teacher.

He: A member of human systems and an eager learner.

Scene 1 describes the consequences of relational blindness.
Scene 2 deals with the transformation or relational blindness into relational sight.

Scene 1
Relational Blindness

17 What About All the Drama?

She says she's a scientist, a student of organization. She's been interviewing me now for several hours. I've been telling her all about this organization—about my boss, my work, our special High Zest Initiative, the meetings I had today, our new products, the current challenges. As I'm talking, I'm struck by one thing: *she's not taking any notes.* What kind of scientist is this? But I go on. I tell her the details: the battles I'm having with Charley, the various personality quirks of all the players—the bosses, the managers, the supervisors, the workers. Still no notes. I tell her about our new Instant Gratification Plan for customers. No notes. Then I review minute-by-minute all of the events of the day and the week. Then we go over the year. Still no notes. Then it's over.

"Is that all?" she says.

"That's about it," I say.

She takes out her clipboard and checks off one box.

"What's that?" I ask.

"My summary," she answers.

"Your summary?" I exclaim. "One check mark!"

"That's it," she says.

"What have you checked?" I ask.

"DBR," she says.

"DBR?"

"Yes."

id that's all?"

at's all."

ter all the details I gave you? All the drama. The personality
s. The crises. The breakthroughs. That's all you have to say.
I ask incredulously.

, that covers it pretty well."

"Well, just what is this DBR?" I ask.

"It's the Dance of Blind Reflex," she says. "And thank you very
much."

18 The Dance of Blind Reflex

☐ Check here if DBR. (See definition below.)

☐ Check here if *chronic* DBR. (Pattern persists throughout all
seasons and despite frequent reorganizations and other shuffling of personnel.)

☐ Check here if *episodic* DBR. (Other patterns prevail, but
when trouble hits, the organization falls into DBR.)

Executive Summary

In the Dance of Blind Reflex:

- Tops feel *burdened* by unmanageable complexity.

- Bottoms feel *oppressed* by insensitive higher-ups.

- Middles feel *torn*—they become weak, confused, fractionated, with
no minds of their own.

- Customers feel *righteously done-to* (screwed) by an unresponsive system.

- All of the players fall to see their part in creating any of the above

Burdened Tops

- Tops feel *burdened* by overwhelming complexity and responsibility.

- There is too much to do and not enough time to do it.

- There are fast-moving, ever-changing, unpredictable conditions to deal with.

- Tops receive incomplete information, yet decisions must be made. They make decisions but are not sure whether they are the right decisions. They set priorities but are not sure that they are the right priorities.

- Tops feel a heavy responsibility for the system; so many people's fates—and the fate of the organization—rest in their hands.

- Tops look to Middles for support but feel they don't get the support they need. Tops can't get their initiatives down through their Middles; they can't get consistent information up from their Middles; they feel their Middles are too dependent, not entrepreneurial enough.

- Tops feel isolated and out of touch with much of the system.

- There are many important issues Tops know they should be dealing with—visions, missions, long-range planning, employee initiatives—but with all the firefighting, there just never seems to be the time. Tops wake regularly in the night thinking of things they should be doing.

Oppressed Bottoms

- Bottoms feel *oppressed* in the system.

- Others (higher-ups) make decisions that affect their lives in major and minor ways—reorganizations happen to them. Initiatives come and go. Health and retirement benefits are diminished; plants are closed. Work forces are reduced ("They" call it "rightsizing," but Bottoms know better).

- Bottoms feel unseen and uncared for. They see things that are wrong with their situation and with the organization that higher-ups ought be fixing but aren't.

- Bottoms feel isolated in the system: they don't have the big picture, there is no vision they can commit to, they don't see how their work fits into the whole, they don't get feedback on their work.

- Tops are invisible to them except for ceremonial acts (like Christmas visits), which seem patronizing.

- Bottoms feel that Middles add little value—they are uninformed; they may be well-meaning, but they are powerless; they are inconsistent and uneven. (*Why can't those Middles get their act together?*) Even Bottoms who feel central to the system's work—they are skilled, knowledgeable, experienced—feel vulnerable. Anything can happen!

- Much of Bottoms' energy is focused on "Them" (higher-ups); Bottoms are angry at "Them," frustrated by "Them," resentful of "Them," disappointed with "Them."

Torn Middles

- Middles feel *torn* by the system—they feel weak, confused, and powerless.

- They are pulled between the often conflicting needs, requests, demands, and priorities of those above them and those below them.

- Middles are "loners" in the system—not connected with Tops or Bottoms, and not really connected with one another. Thus each Middle faces the stresses of the system alone, unsupported by others.

- Middles are often seen by others as confused and wishy-washy, as having no firm opinions of their own. And Middles have no independence of thought and action; they don't know who they are.

    Some Middles seek their identity by aligning themselves with Tops, internalizing their goals and wishes. They become more Top than Top, thereby alienating themselves from Bottoms.

    Other Middles align themselves with Bottoms, identifying with them and championing their causes, and thus alienating themselves from Tops (who don't see them as sufficiently "managerial").

Still other Middles bureaucratize themselves, creating such hurdles and hoops for others to jump over and through that others tend to avoid them as much as possible.

Finally, there are those Middles who, in trying to be fair, responsive, and even-handed with both Tops and Bottoms—and with all others who make demands on them—simply burn out in the effort.

- Middles receive little positive feedback; they are never doing quite enough for anybody. In time, many Middles internalize this feedback. ("Maybe I'm not as competent as I thought I was.")

Righteously Done-to Customers

- Customers feel *righteously done-to.*

- They are stunned to find that the system treats them more as problems than as opportunities.

- They feel ignored and inadequately attended to. Promises made; promises broken. Explanations. Delays. Excuses. Everything except the quality service they feel they deserve.

- Customers see the system as focused more on itself than on them.

- When Customers make what seem to them to be reasonable requests or demands, they are greeted with hostility, as if they are at fault.

- Sometimes, frustrated Customers:

    Lower their standards and accept what was previously an unacceptable level of quality

    Fool themselves into believing that low-quality service really is acceptable

    Threaten to take their business elsewhere

    Do take their business elsewhere

    Take their business elsewhere, only to find out that they get the same poor service wherever they go

- Customers feel frustrated, angry, betrayed, powerless.

How Do Those Inside the System Explain Their Condition?

Blame is freely shared:

- Bottoms blame their condition on insensitive, callous, uncaring, out-of-touch higher-ups.

- Tops blame their condition on the complexity of the world they are dealing with.

- Middles blame their condition on the conflicting demands of the middle job.

- Customers blame their condition on self-absorbed, insensitive delivery systems.

- Everyone feels justified.

- No one sees his or her part in creating any of this.

■ ■ ■

"So, that's all there is to my rich and complex life?" he asks. **"A single check beside DBR?"**

"That's it," she says.

"But my life seems so unique, so special, so beautifully chaotic."

"That's how it feels from the inside, but from the outside—"

"It's just DBR."

"Exactly," she says.

"Scary," he says.

Scene 2
From Relational Blindness to Relational Sight

19 Three Patterns of Relationship

Over the years, we have studied three patterns of relationship that occur regularly in system life, whether in the family, the classroom, the organization, or the nation. These are Top/Bottom, End/Middle/End, and Provider/Customer.

Top/Bottom

The Top/Bottom relationship is one in which one party—Top—has designated responsibility for the system or piece of the system (the organization, division, department, classroom, meeting, project, and so forth) and the other party—Bottom—is a member within that system (worker, student, faculty member, subordinate, meeting attender, team member, and so forth).

End/Middle/End

The End/Middle/End relationship is one in which two or more parties—Ends—with their separate and sometimes conflicting agendas look to a common party—Middle—to move their agendas ahead. Supervisors, middle managers, department chairs, section heads, and negotiators regularly find themselves as Middles between two or more Ends.

Provider/Customer

The Provider/Customer relationship is one in which one party—Provider—is designated to provide another party—Customer—with quality products or services on time and at the right price.

In each of these relationships, there is the potential for a partnership in which both parties are committed to the success of their shared project or process. However, with great regularity, a dance unfolds that knocks the relationship out of the realm of partnership. And this happens without the parties' awareness or choice. Blind reflex.

20 | One Wakes, the Other Sleeps

So I ask her: "How can you tell if you're a Burdened Top or an Oppressed Bottom?" And she asks me: "How are you sleeping at night?"

How Can I Know When I'm a Burdened Top?

When you wake in the night—
your palms damp,
your heart beating.
You are worrying.
You are thinking about all the people you are letting down,
about all the things you should be doing
that you're not doing,
about all the things you're not doing as well as
you should be doing them.
And all the while you're lying there,
it's crystal clear to you
that everyone else is asleep.

How Can I Know When I'm an Oppressed Bottom?

When all your energy is focused on "Them"—
the higher-ups—
on all the things they're not doing
that they should be doing,
on all the things they are doing
that they shouldn't be doing,
your anger at Them,

your disappointment with Them,
your resentment of Them.
It's crystal clear to you
that whatever is wrong here
is *their* fault.

21 The Top/Bottom Dance of Blind Reflex

Top/Bottom
We are in a variety of Top/Bottom relationships—
sometimes as Top
and sometimes as Bottom.

We are Teacher to Student
or Student to Teacher,

Manager to Worker
or Worker to Manager,
Parent to Child
or Child to Parent,
Team Leader to Team Members
or Team Member to Team Leader,
Meeting Convener to Meeting Attender
or Meeting Attender to Meeting Convener,
Leader to Citizen
or Citizen to Leader.

We are in Top relationships
to certain system members
and in Bottom relationships
to others.

The Possibility of Partnership
When we are in Top/Bottom relationships,
it is possible
and mutually beneficial
to be in partnership
regarding responsibility for
the classroom,
the project,
the meeting,
the team,
the family,
the nation.

However, in the Dance of Blind Reflex,
we fall out of that potential for partnership.

The Top/Bottom Dance of Blind Reflex

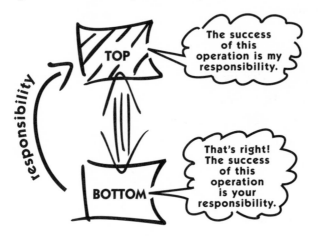

In the Dance of Blind Reflex,
Top becomes increasingly responsible for
the organization,
classroom,
department,
meeting,
team,
family,
nation—
while Bottom becomes decreasingly responsible.

As responsibility shifts to Top
and away from Bottom,
Teacher becomes responsible for the classroom,
Student not responsible;
Manager becomes responsible for the operation,
Worker not responsible;
Meeting Convener becomes responsible for the meeting,
Meeting Attender not responsible;

Parent becomes responsible for the family,
Child not responsible;
Team Leader becomes responsible for the team,
Team Member not responsible;
Leader becomes responsible for the nation,
Citizen not responsible.

And these shifts happen
without awareness or choice
by either Top
or Bottom.

Out of Partnership, But Maybe Not a Problem
Top and Bottom are now out of partnership,
but as long as Top continues to do a great job
that may not be a problem.

Falling Into the Burdened and the Oppressed
But when difficulties arise,
Top falls into burden—
carrying the load of the problem,
feeling like he or she is letting the system down,
worrying—
while Bottom falls into oppression—
holding Top responsible for the failure,
feeling like a blameless sufferer because of Top's inadequacy.

Gradual Disabling of Both
And even if Top continues to do a great job,
there is a gradual disabling of both parties:
an ever-increasing burden on Top

and a growing dependency and incapacity of Bottom.
(What happens when you decide you need Bottom?)

Stepping Out of the Dance of Blind Reflex
Despite its often downgraded reputation,
awareness is everything
(or almost everything).
Seeing the dance gives us the choice:
to continue the dance
or to change it.

As Tops,
we can see ourselves
pulling responsibility
up to ourselves
and away from others,
and we can see Bottoms
turning it over
to us.

As Bottoms,
we can see ourselves
giving responsibility up to Tops,
and we can see them
pulling it up to themselves.

As Tops,
we can choose
to stop pulling responsibility up to ourselves,
and instead
find ways of creating responsibility in others
while remaining responsible ourselves.

As Bottoms,

we can choose

to stop holding Them wholly responsible for the system,

and instead

see ourselves as central players

in the success of this classroom,

department,

organization,

meeting,

family,

team,

nation.

Resistance

Some Tops complain about their burden

while clinging to it.

They fear losing control

when they are still responsible

(a not unreasonable fear);

they fear that others won't be as responsible

or as skilled

or as committed as they are.

They are concerned that creating responsibility in others—

involving them,

training them,

developing them—

takes too much time.

It is easier to simply do it yourself.

And some Tops simply accept burden

as being part of the job.

With awareness comes choice,

and some Tops choose burden.

And some Bottoms complain about their oppression

while clinging to it.

They complain about the insensitivity

and incompetence

of Tops

and about the negative consequences these have

for the classroom,

team,

organization,

department,

meeting,

family,

nation,

but refuse to accept their roles as central players

in the success

or failure

of the system.

"Why should I? I'm just a Bottom."

"They get paid to take the heat."

With awareness comes choice,

and some Bottoms choose oppression.

Partners in Creation

In the Dance of Blind Reflex,

Tops are the owner of the system,

and Bottoms are the recipients of it.

The challenge in stepping out of the Dance
is for Tops and Bottoms—
each side bringing its unique
experiences,
knowledge,
and skills—
to become cocreators of the system—
the classroom,
the team,
the department,
the organization,
the meeting,
the family,
the nation,
the world;
sharing responsibility
for its successes
and its failures
in each moment
and in the long term.

■   ■   ■

He: That is a beautiful dance, isn't it?

She: How do you mean?

He: It all fits so nicely together. The more Top plays Top, the easier
it is for Bottom to play Bottom. And vice versa.

She: Exactly. And what makes it especially compelling is that neither
party realizes it is doing anything. It's all blind reflex. Top is
burdened, Bottom is oppressed, and that's the way it is. No one
does anything. It's simply the way things are. Or so it seems.

He: So how do we avoid the dance?

She: First, we see it.

He: And then?

She: And then we choose: Continue the dance or try a new dance.

He: That seems straightforward.

She: We shall see.

22 It Takes Two to Tango . . . or Does It?

She has a conversation with Top and Bottom:

Bottom: I'd assume responsibility if Top would let it go.

Top: I'd let it go if Bottom would take it on.

Bottom: I'd do my part if only Top would do its.

Top: Everyone knows: You can't make someone responsible.

Top and Bottom: It takes two to tango; that's obvious.

She: If the two agreed, that would be nice. It would make for change, smooth and easy.

Top and Bottom: That's what it takes.

She: But what if only one chooses to change the dance?

Top and Bottom: Sorry, it can't be done.

She: Are you sure?

Top and Bottom: It takes two to tango. First principle.

She: What if you began to change the dance yourself?

Top: You'd look darn silly.

Bottom: You'd be left out there dancing all by yourself.

She: And if you kept on dancing?

Bottom: You might get put away.

Top: Or fired.

Bottom: Or yelled at.

She: Is that all?

Top: I suppose after a while you might just give up and go back to the old dance.

She: That's possible. Anything else?

Bottom: It's possible that the relationship would just end. The two could no longer work together.

She: That's also possible. Is there anything else?

Top (reluctantly):   I suppose it's also possible that, in time, the other might choose to join you in the new dance.

She: So that's possible too.

Top and Bottom: So everything's possible. Big deal!

She: Precisely! It is a big deal. Don't you see what you just said?

Top and Bottom: No!

She: When you change the dance, you create possibility—no more, no less. You break the pattern. Everything is up for grabs. The relationship, as it has been, can no longer continue. So now what? You create chaos—a disruption of the energy pattern.

Top: That's a good thing?

She: Good or bad, it's what happens when one chooses to change the dance.

Bottom: It sounds like a mess.

She: So, you'd prefer something neater—an organized transformation, complete with predictable outcomes?

Top: Who wouldn't?

She: Then when the other says "No" to the new dance, you stop. Is that it?

Bottom: It's only sensible.

She: It's not sensible; it's an excuse. "No" is not the end of the process; it is the beginning. It is the sign that the relationship is entering the messy zone of possibility. If you quit, you miss the opening. It is exactly as you have said: If you continue to dance the new dance alone, everything is possible, and when everything is possible, things are a mess: They may put you away; the relationship might end; you might fall back into the old dance; the other might choose to join you in creating a new dance. This is the mess of transformation. Can it be any other way? Think of relationship as energy—settled into a particular pattern, uncomfortable for all parties, yet comfortable in its predictability. And now you disrupt the pattern. Why would you expect that to be a smooth and predictable process? You have created flux, instability. In that instability lies hope—the hope of creating new patterns that will be more satisfactory for all. Don't run away from flux. Work with it. It is the sound of the old dance shaking.

What is power after all?

Power is the ability to act as if you can make happen

whatever it is you want to make happen,

knowing that you cannot

and being willing to work with whatever does happen.

23 Let's Declare Bankruptcy: Transforming the Top/Bottom Dance

When the Dance of Blind Reflex is all there is, it remains invisible to us. It is only when some variation or mutation occurs that one is able to see both the regular pattern and its alternative.

Such a mutation in the Top/Bottom pattern occurred in one of our Organization Workshop exercises. A familiar story was unfolding: Tops were overwhelmed by demands coming at them from Customers, from their Managers, and from Workers. The time pressures were excruciating. The organization was in disarray. There was little patience to be found anywhere. Customers were dissatisfied—seeing the organization as inadequately responsive to their needs. Money was not coming in; consequently, there were few funds for salaries. And Worker complaints were mounting. None of this was unusual, given the complexity of the conditions, but it was what happened next that opened our eyes both to the usual pattern and to the possibility of transformation.

The Tops were meeting in their office. It was painfully clear that the organization was failing. One Top suggested the possibility of declaring bankruptcy. "It's hopeless. There's no point in going on." There was general agreement. Bankruptcy could end this nightmare. "Let's go out there and finish this."

It was at this point that the pattern began to disintegrate—first at the Top, then at the Bottom.

As the Tops were leaving to make their announcement, one Top stopped them. "Why are we deciding this?" he asked. The others were stunned. The question was too far out of the pattern even to be under-stood at first. The Top persisted. "Why is it our decision? Why don't we tell the others the situation and see what they say?"

Even if one did not understand the language, one could see and feel the discombobulation at the top. Confusion. Heated conversation. Conflicting statements—sometimes coming from the same mouth.

"Why are we talking about this?"
"Why not?"
"It's already settled."
"Maybe."
"It's our decision."
"Is it?"

After considerable back and forth, it was agreed: "What's our rush? Let's put the situation to the others and see what happens. What's to lose?"

And so they did. And then the discombobulation at the Bottom:

"You Tops screwed up."
"What can we do?"
"I guess it's over."
"Is it?"
"Why bother us with this? It's your business."
"It's our business."
"It's hopeless."
"We can fix it."
"It's dead."
"Not yet it isn't."
"Now what?"
"Let's stop."
"Let's go on."

A messy time. Confusing. "What are we to do? The past is no guide for us." Out of the mess a new form emerged. The organization wasn't dead. There was no bankruptcy. There was a shift in energy throughout the organization and among its Customers. There was new commitment to making this thing work. A culture change. Projects were completed; money came in; salaries were paid.

Not everyone was swept up in this culture change. Some Workers remained committed to their traditional Bottomness—whining, complaining, feeling put-upon, more committed to holding Tops responsible than to success—just as there was some feeling at the Top that involvement of the Workers—although it saved the organization—was an admission of Top failure.

And so we step back from the event. What happened here? The mutation reveals quite clearly both the pattern and its alternative. The Big Issue hits. It's crystal clear to Top that Top decides. Just as it's equally clear to Bottom that Top decides (assuming Bottom ever hears about the issue, which is itself unlikely until it is too late to do anything about it). Then the mutation. The shift that fundamentally transforms our world: *Can we be in partnership around the life of this system?*

artnership:

A relationship in which

we are jointly committed

to the success of

whatever endeavor, process, or project

we are engaged in

The term *partnership* is much abused, but isn't that what we are talking about? Even though we are in a Top/Bottom relationship, isn't it in our mutual interest to be in partnership about the life of this system? this organization? this classroom? this project? this meeting? wherever we are prone to falling into the traditional pattern? And if we are truly in partnership over the life of this system, haven't we fundamentally transformed this Top/Bottom relationship?

He: It seems to me you're talking about a lot more than just life in the organization. This Top/Bottom stuff is everywhere—the community, the government, the world.

She: Isn't it.

He: When I think about being Bottom, it strikes me as a painfully comfortable place.

She: That's an interesting phrase—"painfully comfortable."

He: But that's just what it is. I have all of my complaints about "Them"—the mayor, the city government, the president, the world leaders—all these things that they're doing wrong, all the aggravation they're causing me. At the same time there's something very comfortable about having them to blame.

She: It would be quite a project to turn that around, wouldn't it?

24 The Universal Civics Course

This business of trusting or distrusting Tops is truly a phony issue. It's as if the issue is about their trustworthiness. But the issue of system membership is not about "Them," it is about "Us." How trustworthy are we as members and citizens? Are we, even as lowly members, willing to accept our roles as cocreators of our systems? When we say "I trust and support the Tops," isn't that an easy way to step away from our responsibility for this system? Isn't that simply a prelude to my blaming

"Them" when the system fails?

When the leaders' grand visions turn to ashes—as they so often do—we kick the bums out, impeach them, send them into exile, hang them, or shoot them. And then we wait. We wait for the next leader whom we can again hold responsible for our lives and our systems. And on and on it goes.

There are two parallel myths about leaders. The first is that all progress comes from the actions of enlightened leaders; the second is that all the horrors of humanity—warfare, oppression, genocide—are attributable to demonic leadership.

These myths are comforting to us as system members in that they absolve us of responsibility for both progress and disaster. However, they do not reflect historical truth. The eight-hour workday was not arrived at because factory owners thought it would be a nice thing to do. The advance of women was not the result of men deciding it was high time to give the ladies a fair shake. Nor did the end of slavery happen because slaveholders and the government decided that freedom was a legitimate right of all people. In all cases, progress occurred not out of the benevolence and wisdom of leaders, but out of the messy, impudent, and relentless pushback—through strikes, demonstrations, resistance, and civil disobedience—of system members.

And it also is true that oppression, warfare, and holocausts have existed only through the acquiescence of the members.

Which brings us to the Universal Civics Course.

civics *(ˈsi-viks) n. The study of government dealing with the rights and duties of citizens.*

The rights and duties of citizens. Now there's an interesting idea!

I propose that we develop a Universal Civics Course. Its purpose will be to enlighten all of us regarding our rights and duties as members/citizens.

In the course we will explore the role not only of the leaders but also of the members in humankind's history of warfare, oppression, and genocide: How the members trusted too much. How they abandoned their own responsibility. How they were too lazy to work at citizenship. How they went for the bait when their leaders told them how special and noble and deserving they were in contrast to the others, in contrast to "Them." How they found easy targets for their frustrations. How they insisted on reserving the good life for themselves while others were surrounded by evil and injustice. How they fought with one another instead of pushing back at the leaders.

We will study case after case—from the past and the present—of this pattern of member complicity in evil. And then the first phase of the course will end.

The Final Examination

Some years later, the Leader will call our Graduates out to war.

"Our cause is noble," the Leader will say. "We want nothing for ourselves, only justice for others.

"The enemy is the Devil, set on our destruction," the Leader will say. "Our people are great. We have not started this war, nor do we want it. But our personal wishes must be set aside in the face of this great threat. To war, boys and girls, to war! Our cause is just!"

Our graduates will listen to the Leader. They will study the facts. They will dig deep—behind the propaganda. They will observe the Leader closely: They will see all the tricks the Leader uses to arouse their emotions and dampen their minds. ("Notice that chill that runs up and down your spine. Isn't it great how the Leader does that?") They have seen all of this before. They will study, observe, discuss, and when the Leader speaks, they will listen hard.

Then they will look at one another; smiles will break out across their faces; there will be giggles, then laughter, then wave after wave of bent-over-double, helpless, uncontrollable laughter.

And then the difficult business of cocreation will begin, which is the final examination for the Universal Civics Course.

Who Wants the Universal Civics Course?

Does anyone in power want the Universal Civics Course? Think about it. You're the owner of your business or the Top

Executive of your company or the parent in the family or the teacher in the classroom or the Leader of the nation. Do you want your members to be cocreators? How can I even begin to create the Universal Civics Course if my students insist on being cocreators? Wouldn't we much prefer that our members trust us to do the right thing?

It is naive to expect leaders to encourage the development of the Universal Civics Course. Maybe that's the way it should be. The rights and duties of citizens are the members' business.

25 The End/Middle/End Dance of Blind Reflex

And sometimes

we are in End/Middle/End relationships:

Sometimes as Middle between two or more Ends

who look to us for support on their separate agendas;

and sometimes as an End

looking to the Middle for support of our agenda.

And when we are blind to this relationship,

we are in danger of falling into the dance of

the Unsupported End

and the Torn Middle.

End/Middle/End

In the End/Middle/End relationship,
two or more parties, Ends—
with their separate and sometimes conflicting agendas—
are looking to a common party, Middle,
to move their separate agendas ahead.
In organization life,
we are in a variety of End/Middle/End relationships:
Sometimes as an End
and sometimes as a Middle.

Some of our End/Middle/End relationships are vertical:

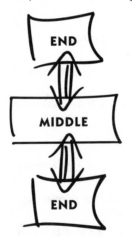

We are Supervisors between Workers
and Managers;
we are Department Chairs
between Faculty
and Administration.

Other End/Middle/End relationships are horizontal:

We are Negotiators between
one party
and another;
we are Managers
between Customers
and Producers.

And some End/Middle/End relationships are *group-to-group*:

We are the Procurement organization
between Suppliers
and Manufacturers.

The Possibility of Partnership

In End/Middle/End relationships,
it is possible and mutually beneficial for us to function in
partnership
in moving ahead Ends' agendas.

However, in the Dance of Blind Reflex,
we fall out of that potential for partnership.

The End/Middle/End Dance of Blind Reflex

In the End/Middle/End Dance of Blind Reflex,
Ends become decreasingly responsible
for resolving their own issues and conflicts,
while Middle becomes increasingly responsible
for resolving these.

And this happens without the awareness
of either Ends
or Middle.

As this shift occurs,
Ends make demands on Middle
that seem simple enough to the Ends
("Any competent Middle should be able to handle this"),
but that Middle finds most difficult to meet
while still feeling responsible for meeting them.

Out of Partnership, But Maybe Not a Problem

Ends and Middle are out of partnership,
but as long as Middle continues to do a great job meeting
both Ends' needs
there may not be a problem.

Falling Into the Unsupported and the Torn

But when Middle fails to deliver,
we can see how Ends fall into being unsupported
("Why am I stuck with such a weak and ineffectual
Middle?"),
while Middle falls into being torn

("My work is important—I am needed by both sides—but I can't seem to please anyone. Maybe I am weak . . . confused . . . ineffective . . incompetent").

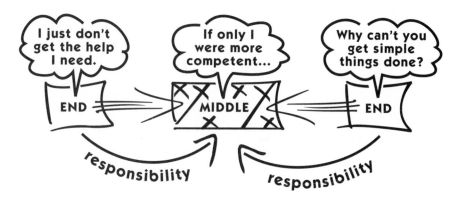

Gradual Disabling of Both

Even if Middle continues to deliver for both Ends,
there is a gradual disabling of both parties,
with Middle burning out
while Ends grow increasingly incapable of handling their own issues.

Stepping Out of the Dance

With awareness comes the possibility of choice.

As Ends, we can become aware;
we can see ourselves
shifting responsibility
for resolving issues and conflicts
from ourselves
to Middle.

We can see ourselves
holding Middle responsible
for accomplishments
that we would find difficult, if not impossible, for ourselves.

As Middles, we can become aware;
we can see ourselves
taking on full responsibility
for resolving Ends' issues and conflicts.

As Middles, we need to find ways
of involving Ends more directly
in resolving *their own* issues and conflicts.
As Ends, we need to become more directly involved
in resolving our own issues and conflicts.

Resistance

Some Middles,
while complaining about the condition of being torn,
cling to it.
They enjoy being in the middle—
needed by both sides—
so central,
so important.
("What would I be if I weren't in the middle?")

And some Ends,
while complaining about the condition of being
unsupported,
cling to it.
It's nice not having to do those difficult things oneself;
it's nice having Middle to blame when things go wrong.

With awareness comes choice:
What do we want?
Importance?
Ease?
Someone to blame?
Or
moving one's agenda ahead?
It's our choice.

Partners in Conflict Resolution

In the Dance of Blind Reflex,
Middles are responsible
for resolving Ends' issues and conflicts;
Ends are not.

The challenge in stepping out of the dance
is for each party to bring its unique resources to bear.
Ends are the central players;
it is *their* issues that need to be resolved,
their agendas that need to be moved ahead.
To this process, Middle brings its unique perspective—
not the perspective of one End
or the other,
but Middle's own view.
And Middle brings tools
that support Ends
in working out their issues.

■　■　■

He: This is gonna be tough. *They want me in the middle!*

She: First, be clear that your job is to help them resolve their issues and conflicts.

He: Why do they need me?

She: To use your skills and your perspective to help them deal with the issues they are facing.

He: They want me to do it for them.

She: And your job is to get them in partnership around resolving their own issues.

He: Partnership again! It's getting clearer to me that this partnership business you keep talking about is a most unnatural act.

She: There's always the dance to fall back on. And keep in mind that you're not the one who is always in the middle. Sometimes you're the End who is making unreasonable demands of Middle. So think about partnership from that angle.

He: Oh!

26 Daniel: Mutant in the Middle Space

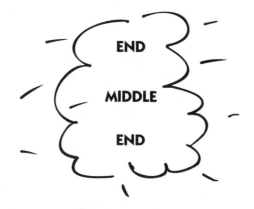

Sometimes the pain of the dance becomes so excruciating for one party that it leads that party to unilaterally break out of the dance into the *possibility* of transformation. Such was the case with Daniel.[1]

Daniel had been a Middle in one of our Power Labs. The End/Middle/End dance had been going on vigorously for several days. Tops and Bottoms had been holding Daniel responsible for resolving their own issues, and Daniel had been pulling that responsibility up to himself. Both Tops and Bottoms were dissatisfied with Daniel's performance: to the Bottoms, he was too weak, wishy-washy, a mindless lackey of the Tops, and to the Tops, he was indecisive, lacking a "managerial mentality." Despite the abuse and lack of support from both sides, Daniel persisted: working morning to night, committed to keeping this system from falling apart, feeling that this was his responsibility.

Then something snapped. Without warning Daniel dropped out of the society. He stopped caring about the Tops and Bottoms. He spent his days by the pool reading. He resisted all efforts to bring him back into the society—into the middle. He never did reenter. And, despite others' treating him as a dropout ("What lesson do you learn from this, Daniel?"), he felt terrific.

But this is only part one of the story. When Daniel returned to his "back-home" job, he immediately found himself right back in the middle. His Bottoms were unhappy about some new arrangements made by his Tops. The Bottoms wanted Daniel to come down, hear their complaints, and then fix it up with the Tops. For that is how the dance usually went—with Daniel in the middle between the Tops (as one End) and the Bottoms (as the other); with Daniel feeling very important and central to the situation, carrying messages from one End to the other, explaining one side to the other, never doing quite enough for either side, and so on. But something popped and the dance was interrupted and the possibility of transformation began to unfold; first for Daniel, then in his interactions with Bottoms, then in those with Tops, and finally in their interactions with one another.

We do not know Daniel's precise thoughts when he was first approached by the Bottoms, but we suspect it was something like the following: *This is not my problem* (a very important first step). *This is their problem. What I need to do is help* them *work this out with* one another.

So Daniel went to the Bottoms and listened to their issues, but when they instructed him to carry their message to the Tops, he refused. He told them what he would do was set up a meeting between them and the Tops so that they could present their issues directly. He said he would work with them, coach them, support them in making the best case they could, but he made it clear that he would not do it for them.

So now the usual dance began to unravel.

"No, Daniel, you do it."

"Sorry, it's your issue, not mine."

"But you're our Middle; it's your job."

"No, my job is to help you do what you feel needs to be done, but you've got to do it."

Is this resistance? Should Daniel stop because the Bottoms said "No" to his proposal? Or is "No" precisely what one should expect—possibly even look forward to—as the energy pattern of the familiar dance is disrupted?

Daniel persisted, and the Bottoms finally agreed that, with Daniel's coaching, they would take their case to the Tops.

A parallel process occurred when Daniel brought this proposal for a face-to-face meeting to the Tops.

The sounds of the dance breaking up:

"We're too busy."

"It's important that you hear directly from them."

"That's what we hired you to do."

"You hired me to use my best judgment."

When the Top says "No," is it the end of the conversation or the beginning? Or is "No" simply the sound of the familiar dance shaking?

For Daniel, "No" was the beginning of the conversation; he persisted, and the Tops agreed to the meeting.

Daniel coached the Bottoms. The meeting was held. It was awkward at first but quickly developed into a productive encounter. Tops and Bottoms worked out a satisfactory resolution of their issues. Both sides felt it was a good meeting. Daniel commented that he had "the driest palms in the room" (palmar perspiration count may be an objective measure of where responsibility lies).

The shift was toward partnership. *Middle did not abdicate responsibility.* Daniel remained committed to the resolution of this issue, but he made it clear, first to himself and then to others, that this was not his issue but theirs, and that both Ends must be in full partnership around its resolution.

Some might see this shift as diminishing the role of Middle. This is clearly not the case. For Daniel, it opened up a whole new realm of possibility about what it meant to be Middle. "I began to look around and ask myself: 'What's not happening that could be happening? Who are the people who need to be together to make it happen? How can I get them together and support their interaction with one another?'"

Yet even after this highly productive meeting between Daniel's Tops and Bottoms, there were lingering pressures to restore the old dance. Immediately following the meeting, when all the others had left the room, the Top of the Tops said to Daniel: "Great meeting, Daniel." And then, after a pause, "But don't you ever do it again."

So for Daniel—and for all the rest of us Daniels out there—is "No" no, or is it the continuing echo of the traditional End/Middle/End dance shaking?

27 Organizations in the Middle

The End/Middle/End dance is not limited to interactions among individuals. It also takes place among organizational groups. Take, for example, the situation faced by a worldwide Procurement organization. Their job was to purchase parts and equipment from Suppliers for use by Manufacturing. There was considerable confusion within Procurement as to what their role was, and there were constant complaints from both Suppliers and Manufacturing.

Manufacturing was constantly after Procurement to reduce costs. ("We're under pressure to keep our costs down. You [Procurement] account for over 60 percent of our costs. Do better!")

And the Suppliers felt vulnerable. They wanted long-term relationships with the company and were willing to meet all sorts of price and process demands to make that possible. Suppliers were constantly adjusting but still felt vulnerable.

Procurement felt that Manufacturing was difficult to deal with; they made unreasonable demands and were unwilling to get involved in what they thought were Procurement's problems.

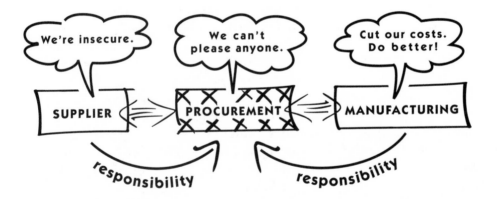

Once the Director of Procurement saw that the department was caught up in a classical End/Middle/End dance, the choice became clear: We can continue to assume *full* responsibility for procurement or we can work to move some of that responsibility out to Manufacturing and the Suppliers.

The decision was made to change the role of Procurement from *doing* procurement to *facilitating the procurement relationship* between Supplier and Manufacturing.

There was initial resistance from Manufacturing ("Procurement is your job") and from some people within Procurement, as *facilitating* procurement seemed less powerful and less significant than *doing* procurement (despite the aggravation that regularly accompanied the doing).

Is resistance *resistance* or merely the sound of the old dance shaking? The Director persisted. "Responsibility is now where it belongs. Our business is to put Suppliers and Manufacturing together. That's where the issues of Supplier security and Manufacturing costs are best handled."

28 The Provider/Customer Dance of Blind Reflex

And sometimes

we are in Provider/Customer relationships:

sometimes as Provider

and sometimes as Customer.

And when we are blind to this relationship,

we are in danger of falling into the dance of

the Unfairly Judged Provider

and the Done-to Customer.

Provider/Customer

In organization life,
we are in a variety of Provider/Customer relationships:
Sometimes as Provider—
designated to provide some service or product to another
person or group,
and sometimes as Customer—
the seeker of some high-quality product or service from the
Provider.

The Possibility of Partnership
When we are in Provider/Customer relationships,
it is possible
and mutually beneficial
for us to be in partnership
regarding the delivery of high-quality products and services.

In the Dance of Blind Reflex, however,
we regularly fall out of that potential for partnership.

The Provider/Customer Dance of Blind Reflex
In the Dance of Blind Reflex,
Provider becomes increasingly responsible
for the delivery of the product or service,
and Customer becomes decreasingly responsible.

As responsibility shifts,

delivery becomes the Provider's business

and entitlement becomes the Customer's.

And this happens without awareness

of either Provider

or Customer.

■   ■   ■

He: Wait a minute! Stop the dance. There's something seriously wrong here.

She: What's wrong?

He: Look, I had no problem seeing the Top/Bottom shift. The End/Middle/End shift caused me a little more difficulty. *But this!* This is going too far. Customers are entitled. That's what it is to be Customer.

She: So what happens when the Customer gets unsatisfactory delivery?

He: *The Customer's not supposed to get unsatisfactory delivery!*

She: Right. But what happens when that's what they get?

He: I suppose you get mad, you complain, and you might even find yourself another supplier.

She: Exactly. And what don't you get?

He: (*pondering*) I guess the thing you don't get is delivery.

She: Exactly. You get anger, you get frustration, and you get a solid dose of righteous indignation. What you don't get is delivery. So the question is: What matters more to you? Delivery or righteous indignation?

He: (*whining*) *But it's the Provider's fault!*

She: I guess your answer is righteous indignation.

■   ■   ■

Out of Partnership, But Maybe Not a Problem

In the dance,

Provider and Customer are out of partnership,

but as long as Provider continues to provide high-quality
service

that may not be a problem.

Falling Into the Righteously Done-to and the Unfairly Judged

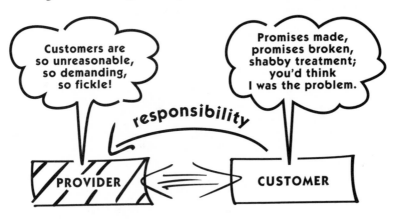

But when quality delivery fails to materialize,

Customer falls into being the Done-to:

"Look at this poor delivery!

It's your fault.

I'm the Customer;

I deserve better."

And Provider falls into being the Unfairly Judged:

"We did the best we could.

The Customers make unreasonable demands;

they are fickle, disloyal.

They don't know what's good for them;

they don't understand our constraints;
they don't appreciate what a fine job we've done."

Gradual Disabling of Both

And even if Provider continues to provide quality delivery,
there is a gradual disabling of both parties—
Provider burning out
and Customer lulled into a false sense of security (ill-
equipped to handle problems and getting less than Customer
could get with involvement).

Partners in Delivery

It is possible
and desirable
for Provider
and Customer
to be in partnership in the delivery process.
Customer needs to share responsibility for the delivery
process.
("If I don't get what I want, then I'm also to blame.")
Customer needs to become more directly involved in the
delivery process—
knowing how the delivery system works;
setting clear demands and standards;
getting into the delivery process early as a partner,
not late as a judge;
staying close to the Provider.
And the Provider needs to allow the Customer into the
delivery process.

■   ■   ■

He: You can bet there'll be resistance on this one. Does the Customer want to be responsible? Does the Provider want the Customer messing around in the Provider's business?

She: There will be resistance, which is why we have so much poor delivery and so many Righteously Done-to Customers and Unfairly Judged Providers. But is resistance just resistance? Isn't it also the sound of the old dance breaking up? Isn't it also the harbinger of the possibility of transformation?

He: Or else it's the Dance of Blind Reflex.

She: Exactly.

29 Overcontrol or Transformation: The Mutant Customer

There is much talk about the need for "paradigm shifts"—fundamentally different models for comprehending human behavior in social systems. It is difficult, however, to recognize such shifts, even when they are directly in front of us. The difficulty is this: We view the new through the old lens and, as a consequence, we look without seeing. Consider the following example from the Organization Workshop.

The usual Customer pattern is unfolding. The Customers, having made their presentations to Tops regarding their needs and requirements, are now waiting patiently in their offices for results. They sit and wait.

Not all Customers are waiting, however. Sandra is making quite a pain in the neck of herself. She is constantly at the Tops' offices making new demands. The Tops keep assuring her that her project is in good hands and well under way, but that's not good enough for Sandra. She wants more involvement. The Tops see her as an interference. Sandra wants to have some say in who works on her project. She wants to meet directly with the Workers. She is not satisfied simply getting progress reports from Middles or Tops. She insists on being right in there with the Workers.

Sandra is looking a bit strange to the other Customers—pushy, lacking trust in the process. Apparently Sandra cares little for the other Customers' reactions; she persists. The Tops try to hold her off, but Sandra is not to be stopped. In the end she gets her way: She meets the Workers; she gets involved in selecting the team to work on her project; she engages directly with the team, meeting regularly with team members.

Program staff have been observing all of this: Sandra's "pushiness," the discomfort she is producing in Tops and Middles, her unrelenting drive for involvement. One staff member comments: "That's Sandra, with her inordinate needs for control." Other staff nod in agreement. It's clear to all that that's what they're dealing with here—an inordinate need for control.

There are other results that indicate that something beyond "control needs" is going on here. Other Customers complain about the service they get: Promises are made but not kept; delivery is late; products are substandard. It is clear to these Customers that the organization has failed them. Sandra, however, is delighted with her results: She gets surprisingly good products; she enjoys interacting directly with the Workers, and they enjoy her. It seems that only management and the staff have problems with Sandra.

What has Sandra done? She changed the dance and in doing so caused the predictable chaos. The other Customers and the Organization are dancing uncomfortably with one another. [Organization: "We are responsible for delivery; you are not." Customers: "You are responsible for delivery; we are not." And when the dance ends, the Organization feels unfairly judged, while the Customers feel righteously done-to.]

Sandra, by contrast, chose to create a different dance. [I am also responsible for delivery.] And she continued that dance in the face of resistance until, in the end, the Organization reluctantly joined in with her.

Through one set of lenses, we see a pattern of personal behavior: Pushiness, overcontrol, lack of trust, and so forth. Through another set of lenses, we see one person transforming the predictable Provider/Customer dance.

30 The Unfairly Judged Professor (and the Righteously Done-to Students)

He takes his teaching responsibilities seriously; he is committed to making a difference in his students' lives. He prepares his syllabus meticulously, with class-by-class activities and assignments, the most relevant and up-to-date readings, illustrative cases, experiential activities. He prepares thoroughly for each class, working hard to draw out his students, engaging them, encouraging them, challenging them.

Some days are better than others, but all in all he is feeling good about the work he is doing and about his vocation as a professor. And then it hits! *The student evaluations*. The evaluations are for the most part positive, some very positive. There are 5's on a five-point scale, with notations written in the margins—"best course so far," "appreciated your command of the material," and so forth. But then there are the others, the 2's and 3's, along with the comments—"too shallow," "too many hours wasted in class discussion," "not enough substance from the professor," "I was expecting more." The professor draws little solace from the positive evaluations, the 3.9 overall rating, the glowing comments from several students. What keeps him up at night and continues to trouble him during the day are those 2's and 3's, the negative comments, the criticisms and complaints, and, worst of all, the fact that he was blindsided, because none of this came to the surface during the life of the course.

So here we have an all-too-familiar classroom tale: the Righteously Done-to Student ("I paid my money, I came to class, I was entitled to a solid education, and you, Professor, didn't deliver.") And on the other side, we have the Unfairly Judged Professor ("I worked my tail off, I did my research, I put together the best course I could, I gave it my all, and never did I hear a word of complaint. And this is the response I get! *Unfair!*")

In the university classroom, no less than in all our other social systems, we exist in relationship with one another, yet when it comes to evaluations, our focus tends to be on the individuals and not on the relationship; the professor evaluates (grades) the student, and then it is the student's chance to evaluate the professor. In all of this, *the*

Provider/Customer relationship goes unnoticed.

Once our attention shifts from individuals to the relationship, then we begin to focus not only on the attributes of the parties, but also on the qualities of the relationship. In the case of the professor/student relationship, the question is, Is that relationship characterized by a joint commitment to the success of the educational venture?

It may seem eminently reasonable for professor and student to be in partnership with one another, to be jointly committed to the success of their educational venture, yet that is not how it often goes in the professor/student relationship, just as in most other Provider/Customer relationships. The more familiar pattern is the responsibility dance, in which responsibility for success resides primarily, if not exclusively, with the professor and minimally, if at all, with the student. Professor is responsible, Student not responsible.

The absence of partnership in and of itself may not be a problem. The Provider professor may take up all responsibility for the course and discharge it brilliantly, and the Customer students who have felt no responsibility for the course still emerge as delighted customers. No problem.

But now let us observe what happens in this nonpartnership pattern when delivery is less than satisfactory. Our nonresponsible student becomes the Righteously Done-to Customer ("You, Professor, were responsible; I was entitled; and you let me down.") And our responsible professor becomes the Unfairly Judged Provider ("I gave it my best; I taught a good course; your reaction is unfair.")

The student can, with impunity, blame the professor for the failure of the course, but the professor cannot blame the student, for if the responsibility dance is on, it is clear that the professor alone is responsible. (The grade the professor gives the student is an evaluation of the degree of mastery of the course content, most likely *not* of the student's contribution to partnership.)

We are stuck with relationship, but do we want partnership? Democracy is not a requirement in the classroom. There have been many great professors who have taught many great courses in which there have undoubtedly been many disgruntled students, yet no one would have thought it necessary, much less appropriate, to have the students evaluate the professors. The teacher taught and the students coped as best they could. But once we choose democracy in the classroom, then the game shifts and partnership becomes relevant. Now we are in this together—and under these conditions it is as valid for the professor to evaluate the student's contribution to partnership as it is for the student to evaluate the professor's.

The professor's evaluation of the student's contribution to partnership might comprise such comments as

- You were a failure as a customer.

- Where were your complaints during the course, when we still might have had the opportunity to deal with them?

- Did you ask me to clarify points you didn't understand?

- Did you speak up when you thought student conversations were dragging on too long?

- Did you suggest topic areas that you expected to be covered, which were not?

And so on.

Professor/student is a systemic relationship. Our choice is whether or not to create it as a partnership relationship. As a professor I may not want that partnership; like many providers, I may not welcome the intrusion of the customer into what I consider my business. And as a student, I may not welcome the opportunity of partnership; like many customers, I may be firmly rooted in my entitlement and not feel that it is my business to help the provider deliver the service I expect. What can drive us toward partnership would be our common interest in creating the best possible product, service, learning experience. And if our choice is not to work on building partnership into the relationship, then we can expect occasional if not frequent bouts of "unfairly judged" and "righteously done-to."

Some professors work to create partnership in the classroom by having an initial contracting session with students, clarifying what each expects from the other. Relationship, however, is an ongoing process, and if our focus is on partnership, then we need to come back regularly to examine that relationship. Is the Provider professor opening him- or herself to evaluations, suggestions, and reactions from the students? And is the Customer student making it clear to the professor what is and is not working in that process? Are we jointly committed to the success of this educational venture?

The Dance of Blind Reflex: Summary

We are constantly shifting in and out of these three relationships:

Top/Bottom

End/Middle/End

Provider/Customer.

In each relationship, it is mutually beneficial for us to be in partnership with one another.

However (not always, not every time, but with great regularity), responsibility flows

from Bottom to Top

from Ends to Middle

from Customer to Provider.

And that is the end of partnership.

This may not be a problem so long as Top, Middle, and Provider continue to deliver.

But when they fail to deliver, we fall into being

burdened Tops and oppressed Bottoms,

torn Middles and disappointed Ends

unfairly judged Providers and righteously

done-to Customers,

and our potential contributions to one another and to our systems are greatly diminished.

He: Hmm!

She: What is it?

He: I'm beginning to see another side to this.

She: And?

He: I'm often in a service role in my organization. Doesn't that put me into a Provider/Customer relationship with my clients?

She: It sure does.

He: And that's what I'm wondering about. Am I the Provider taking on all the responsibility for service? And are my Customers pushing all the responsibility for service onto me? And am I letting that happen?

She: It's hard not to, isn't it?

He: I think it is happening.

She: Ah, the Space of Service. It's a minefield!

He: Try dancing through a minefield.

31 Abused and Misused in the Space of Service

The Service Provider Enters the Space of Service

I am the Service Provider—

the staff specialist,

the technical advisor,

the consultant,

the field service specialist,

the human resources resource,

the therapist—
I enter the Space of Service.
I have my expertise.
I know much about that
but little about this particular situation.
What's unique here?
Where are the minefields?
Whose agendas am I serving?
Whose agendas are being ignored?
What is the history of this situation?
What are people looking for?
Instant solutions?
Painless solutions?
Are some skeptical,
others hopeful,
still others hopeless?
Whatever,
they all look to me.

The Service Provider Needs to Be of Immediate Value
I am the Service Provider.
I enter the Space of Service.
It is crystal clear to me:
I must be of immediate value.
It is crystal clear to my clients:
I must be of immediate value.

The Service Provider Becomes the Expert
I am the Service Provider.
I must be of immediate value.
I am the expert;

I have the solution to your problem,
the system to fix your system,
the process,
the theory,
the tools.
I am the answer to your prayers.

Or . . .

The Service Provider Becomes the Servant

I am the Service Provider.
I must be of immediate value.
I am your servant;
whatever you ask, I do.
The help you request
is the help I give;
the solution you seek
is the solution you receive.
And I empty wastebaskets, too.

The Service Provider "Experts" and "Servants"

I expert you,
I servant you.
The more I expert
and the more I servant,
the less I illuminate,
the more I confuse.
What does your system need?
Really need?

The Service Provider Is Abused and Misused

I am the Service Provider.
Expert or servant,
I come away unclean—
abused,
misused,
of no real value,
my true expertise untapped,
your real needs unaddressed.
I took you and your system
where *I* wanted to go
or where *you* wanted to go
and not where *it* needed to go.

The Service Provider Takes a Stand

I am the Service Provider,
and you are the Client.
My stand is to be
of real and lasting value to this system,
so that it will be a more empowered system
after I am gone.
I have no instant solution.
Can you handle that?
Can I?
I have my expertise,
and you have yours.
Let us use our expertise.
Let us learn together
to understand this system,

appreciate its possibilities,

strengthen it,

move it ahead

in partnership.

■　　■　　■

He: This makes sense to me. I don't enjoy being the servant, and I don't like being the expert, and I do like the idea of being in partnership with my clients, being committed to learning together, being committed to providing the best service possible. But . . .

She: But they won't like it?

He: Exactly.

She: And they'll resist. They might say "No." They might threaten to take their business elsewhere. In fact, they just might do that—find themselves some other willing expert or servant. Or you and they might just fall back into the old dance. Or you might succeed in transforming the dance. It's all possible.

He: It certainly will stir things up.

She: Transformation always does. Always. You are rearranging the energy.

He: The sound of the old dance shaking.

She: Exactly.

32 | The Web of Relationships

He: What I'm beginning to see is that my life is a web of patterns of relationships.

Sometimes I'm Top

and sometimes I'm Bottom.

Sometimes I'm the Middle between Ends

and sometimes I'm an End.

Sometimes I'm the Provider

and sometimes I'm the Customer.

And all of these may be going on simultaneously.

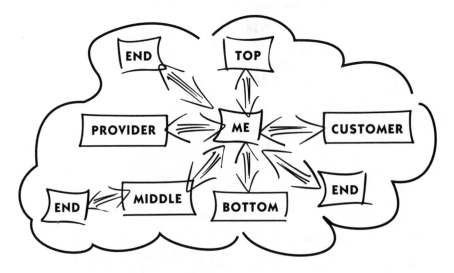

She: And in each relationship, there is the lure of the Dance of Blind Reflex.

He: One party takes on all responsibility for the process, while the other lets it go. It's all so neat.

She: And blind.

He: Partnership . . . it's such an unnatural act.

She: Being jointly committed to the success of whatever one brings to the table.

He: Even if we are in a knock-down, drag-out conflict situation?

She: Especially if we are in a knock-down, drag-out conflict situation.

How to Create Partnership

1. Recognize that we are in relationship: Top/Bottom, End/Middle/End, Provider/Customer, sometimes on one side, sometimes on the other.

2. See the responsibility dance *as it is happening*.

3. Notice where responsibility is: are we pulling it up to ourselves or passing it off to another?

4. Have a vision of an outcome that is better than what currently exists (better service, greater classroom involvement, higher-quality product).

5. Know that we *can* shift the dance and pursue partnership from whatever side of the relationship we are on.

6. Be prepared to persist when we hear "the sound of the old dance shaking."

33 How to Clean Sidewalks: It's a Matter of Being

Skill-training has its place, but what we are exploring here has less to do with skill than with something much more elusive—something that, for the point of this discussion, I'll call *being*.

Skill-training has to do with "doing"—how to do this and how to do that. So let me be clear: I strongly recommend skill-training. If you are to spend time in meetings, it can be very useful to develop greater meeting skills. The same holds true for handling conflicts, dealing with difficult people, brainstorming, problem solving, and myriad other things one must do in order to survive and thrive in systems.

There are, however, many situations in which skill—how to do—is less to the point than being—how to be. Let me take a hypothetical case.

Let us say I am the youngest in the family; my brother is the oldest. Let us say that the two of us live on similar urban streets but in different cities. And let us say that both of us are troubled by—in fact, incensed over—the huge amounts of dog droppings that litter our sidewalks and sometimes find their way onto the bottoms of our shoes. And let us say that both of us have spent considerable time whining and complaining about those inconsiderate dog owners who allow their pets to indiscriminately foul our sidewalks. And let us say that, coincidentally, on the same day my brother and I separately experience epiphanies regarding the dog droppings. Suddenly, it strikes each of us separately that we have been Bottom in the matter of dog droppings. And it strikes us that rather than continue to be victims of this problem, we could be central to making it go away. For both of us this is a liberating and exhilarating thought.

My brother, the firstborn, has proclivities to leadership. I, the lastborn, tend to do things myself. My brother organizes the neighborhood; I go out and buy a huge broom. We both succeed. He and his neighbors work out their methods; I delight in going out periodically with my broom. (Neighbors across the street mistakenly assume I was hired to do the job, so they hire their own dog-dropping technicians.)

Both my brother and I are delighted in our power, in our abilities to convert this complaint into an accomplishment.

Is there a skill to this? Should I learn about community organizing or should my brother learn about broom pushing? I think not. In this, as in so many other cases, we are dealing less with doing than with being. *Once the shift in being occurs, we manage to find our way to doing.* On the other hand, unless there is a shift in being, all the skill-training in the world will not help us.

34 Resistance or The Sound of the Old Dance Shaking

Systems are not simply collections of individuals,
they are patterns of relationship—
Top/Bottom,
End/Middle/End,
Provider/Customer.
We exist only in relationship—
sometimes on one side,
sometimes on the other.
We dance in relationship,
and in the dance,
we grow apart from one another—
becoming the Burdened
and the Oppressed,
the Unsupported
and the Torn,

the Judged
and the Done-to.
We dance
without seeing the dance.
On the inside
there is no dance,
only our feelings,
our beliefs—
so solid,
so sure,
"Reality,"
the way things *really* are.

Can we change the dance?
Maybe,
maybe not.
Maybe we will go on dancing
to the end of our days—
not seeing one another,
not loving one another,
misunderstanding,
hurting, and destroying one another.

Or maybe we will see the dance.
And maybe we will stop the dance.
And maybe we will create a new dance.

But first,
there will be the sound of the old dance shaking.

35 How We Can See the Dance

He: How can we see the dances when we are in them?

She: We can monitor our own behavior. We can coach one another. We can take a stand for partnership. We can pay attention to our feelings.

Monitoring Our Own Behavior

He: How do we monitor our own behavior?

She: (*showing signs of impatience*) Just pay attention!

He: Excuse me.

She: The light is on. By now you should be able to see for yourself. Simply pay attention to the relationships you are in, wherever you are—in the classroom, the meeting, the task force. Wherever. Are you Top in a Top/Bottom relationship? Or are you Bottom? Are you an End or a Middle? A Provider or a Customer? Notice where the responsibility is flowing. Pay attention. Is the dance on? And if it is, then you have a choice: Continue the dance or create a new one.

He: I'm not sure I'll always see the dance.

She: You may not, but keep looking. You'll get better at it. In the meantime, you can coach others and ask others to coach you.

He: Coach me?

She: Coach you.

Coaching

We sometimes see the dance in others
when they don't see it in themselves;
just as they see the dance in us
when we are still blind to it.

Each of us has the power
to turn on the lights for the other.
The dance is on.
Don't you see it?
You're pulling that responsibility up to yourself
and away from others.

You're taking on all responsibility for the system
and falling into becoming the Burdened Top.
You're taking on all responsibility for resolving their issues
and problems
and falling into becoming the Torn Middle.
You're taking on all responsibility for delivery
and falling into becoming the Unfairly Judged Provider.
Do you see that happening?
Do you want to continue the dance
or try a new dance?
Your choice.

Or . . .

You're shifting responsibility
from yourself to others.
You're holding "Them" totally responsible for the system
and falling into becoming the whiny, Oppressed Bottom.
You're holding Middle totally responsible for resolving your
issues
and falling into becoming the Unsupported End.
You're holding Provider totally responsible for delivery
and falling into becoming the Done-to (Screwed) Customer.
Do you see that happening?

Do you want to continue that dance
or try a new dance?
Your choice.

He: This is tough. You call this coaching; some would call it nagging. Criticism. They would resent it.

She: That's the first response—the reflex. But we can get past that. Pause; take a deep breath; let it in. If we're committed to partnership, we encourage coaching; we welcome it. We build it into our system. Our stand is to create and sustain partnership.

Taking a Stand for Partnership

We, the members of this system, are fully aware that, in our interactions with one another, we regularly find ourselves in Top/Bottom, End/Middle/End, and Provider/Customer relationships. And we are fully sensitive to the lure of the Responsibility Dance in which we fall out of the possibility of partnership and into becoming Burdened Tops, Oppressed Bottoms, Unsupported Middles, Judged Providers, and Righteously Done-to Customers.

Our commitment is to avoid the Dance of Blind Reflex and instead create and maintain partnership with one another in whatever endeavor, project, or process in which we are engaged. We are aware that each of us brings different roles, perspectives, experiences, resources, and skills to the process. Our commitment is to respect and use these differences toward the successful resolution of our joint efforts.

She: And your feelings are often a clue that the dance is on.

Paying Attention to Our Feelings

Our subjective experiences
are not simply personal phenomena;
they are systemic phenomena;
they are clues to our condition within the system.

Burdened? If we are feeling burdened by unmanageable complexity, this may be a clue to us that we are Top in a Top/Bottom relationship and are drawing responsibility up to ourselves and away from others. This awareness opens the possibility of finding ways of creating responsibility in others.

Oppressed? If we are finding much of our energy focused on the Tops—the boss, the president, the politicians, the higher-ups, the parents—if we find ourselves angry at "Them," resentful of "Them," disappointed in "Them," this may be a clue to us that we are Bottom in a Top/Bottom relationship and that we are holding "Them" responsible for our condition and for the condition of the system. This awareness opens the possibility of our examining our own responsibility in the situations in which we are feeling oppressed.

Unsupported? If we are feeling unsupported by a weak and ineffectual associate, this may be a clue to us that we are an End in an End/Middle/End relationship, and that we are holding the Middle responsible for resolving our issues and conflicts. *Could we so easily do what we are expecting our Middle to do?* Such awareness opens the possibility of our taking more responsibility for resolving our own issues.

Can't please anyone? If we are feeling weak and ineffective, like we can't please anyone, this may be a clue to us that we are in a Middle position between two or more Ends, and that we are falling into feeling responsible for resolving *their* issues and conflicts. This opens the possibility of our getting more emotional distance for ourselves and finding ways of involving the Ends in resolving their own issues and conflicts.

Unreasonably judged? If we are feeling judged by an unreasonably demanding Customer, this may be a clue to us that we have been taking on to ourselves full responsibility for Customer Service. Maybe we need to find ways of involving the Customer more in their own delivery process.

Feeling done-to? If we are feeling righteously done-to by an uncaring, unresponsive Provider, this may be a clue to us that we have abandoned all personal responsibility for obtaining quality service for ourselves. Maybe we need to find ways of becoming more involved in the delivery process—helping the delivery system be more responsive to us.

SUMMARY

In this section, we have explored the costs of relational blindness. In system life, we humans are in constantly shifting patterns of systemic relationship with one another. For the most part, this phenomenon of being in systemic relationship is invisible to us. As a consequence, we blindly fall into certain relationship dances leading to personal stress, loss of potential partnership, and diminished contributions to our systems.

We have also explored the possibilities of saying "No" to the old dances and creating more satisfying and more constructive new ones. And we have examined strategies for seeing relationship: being more aware of the dances as we are living them, coaching one another, taking a stand for partnership, and using our feelings as clues to the dance.

SEEING PATTERNS OF PROCESS

Act III

For the most part, we human beings do not see the larger system processes of which we are a part. We see individuals within the system, but we do not see "It"—the whole, the system, the family, the team, the business partnership. We do not see "Its" processes as "It" engages with "Its" environment.

In Act Three we will explore the consequences of that blindness. Our focus will be on peer group relationships—on the interactions *among* Tops, *among* Middles, and *among* Bottoms. We will treat each of these groups as a system within the larger system of the organization. We shall see how each of these systems blindly and reflexively falls into dysfunctional patterns of interaction: Turf Warfare among the Tops; Alienation among the Middles; GroupThink among the Bottoms.

We also will see how, in our blindness to system processes, we tend to politicize these processes—valuing some and disvaluing others. And we will explore the consequences of such politicization.

Our language is of the organization, but the phenomena we will describe extend far beyond the realm of the organization. For example, we will find striking parallels between the experiences of Top Executive teams and those of parent couples, between Middle Manager peer groups and suburban neighbors, between embattled Worker groups and embattled urban neighborhoods, ethnic groups, and nations. Familiar dances—unproductive and destructive—unfold reflexively and without awareness or choice with great regularity. Dancing in the dark.

Once again, we will explore the possibility of transforming system life from warfare to partnership as we move from blind reflex to enlightened choice.

129

But not without the sound of the old dances shaking.

Scene 1 describes the consequences of process blindness.
Scene 2 deals with the transformation of process blindness into process sight.
Scene 3 the politics of system processes
Scene 4 the challenge of robust systems

Scene 1
Process Blindness

---

36 Are You Sure You Have It All?

He: Are you sure you have it all?

She: I'm sure.

He: But I gave you so much information. It can't all be covered by that one little check mark.

She: It's all covered.

He: Well, what about that inside information about our Top Executives, about all the crazy mixed messages we were getting from the top? And how about that so-called "amicable breakup" at the top over so-called "philosophical differences." That's special, no?

She: (*She looks bored.*)

He: Well, what about the Top who took early retirement because of "a long-delayed passion for fly-fishing"?

She: (*No response.*)

He: And the "coffee episode"? That tied us up for weeks. Some units had coffee machines in their areas, others didn't. The hearings we held on the coffee committees.

She: (*She chews the eraser but does not write.*)

He: And that led to all those other issues about unfairness: different salary and bonus treatment . . . the infighting that broke out among our Middle Managers . . .

She: (*Nods her head but still doesn't lift the pencil.*)

He: And the business about the Workers: How they used to be a team, but now half the group doesn't talk to the other half . . .

She: (*stifling a yawn*) It's all covered.

He: I don't get it.

She: You will.

He: It's all part of the dance?

She: That's it.

37 Turf Warfare, Alienation, and GroupThink: The Dance of Blind Reflex Continued

Executive Summary

1. Top group members become territorial and fall into turf battles with one another.

2. Middle group members become alienated from and competitive with one another; they never become a group.

3. Bottom group members become a cohesive entity, and they fall into pressuring one another into conformity or GroupThink.

4. When relationships among group members break down, the explanations are tied to the personal characteristics of the individuals involved.

5. And since the explanations are personal, so are the "solutions": fix, fire, rotate, avoid, separate ("divorce"), control or avoid being controlled, therapize one party or both or all of them.

6. But the fundamental issues keep coming back, because . . .

He: Much that seems personal is not personal.

She: Exactly.

Tops Fall into Turf Battles

The Basic Turf pattern:

- Although Tops are collectively responsible for the whole system, they divide responsibility among themselves.

- Each Top becomes increasingly *responsible for* and *knowledgeable about* his or her own territory and decreasingly responsible for and knowledgeable about the territory of others and the whole.

- Tops become more concerned with what is good for *their* area than for the needs of the system as a whole.

- Instead of being in partnership with one another, Tops feel they need to protect themselves from one another.

Common symptoms of Top Turf issues:

- *Lack of support.* Tops feel unsupported by one another. They feel the need to protect themselves against unwanted incursions into their territory.

- *Status/importance differences.* Some areas of responsibility are considered more important to the operation than others. There are the more important Tops and the less important Tops.

- *Resentment.* Some Tops feel that other Tops are not carrying their fair share of the load.

- *Control battles.* There are struggles over the direction the system as a whole should take: Do we grow quickly or gradually? What is our orientation to our employees (or children)? Are we democratic? Autocratic? Laissez-faire? Do we diversify or stick to our core business? Do we take financial risks or play it conservatively?

- *Relationship breakdowns.* Relationships that began with promise deteriorate. Partners end up not talking to each other, or the relationship ends in separation, "divorce," reorganization. (These promising new reorganizations often end up falling into the same DBR pattern.)

- *System consequences.* Tops send out conflicting messages, causing confusion throughout the system; there is limited cooperation across system lines, with the loss of potential synergies; redundant resources pile up in their separate stovepipes. All of this results in increased internal competition and decreased external competition.

He: That's quite a costly dance.

She: Isn't it, though?

Middle Group Members Become Alienated from One Another

The Basic Alienation pattern:
- Middle groups are nongroups. There is no sense of "We," no common mission or purpose.

- Middles feel isolated from one another. Even when together (for example, in staff meetings), it is as if their energies are drawn away from one another.

- If you ask Middles what group they are part of, they are more likely to mention the groups they service or manage rather than their own peer group.

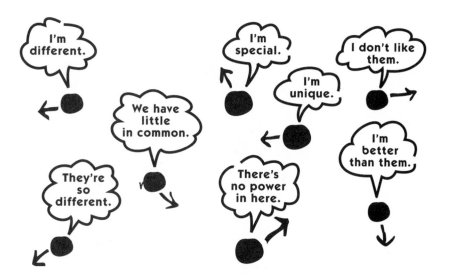

Common symptoms of Middle alienation:

- *Unique.* Middles feel unique, like they have little in common with one another.

- *Competition.* Middles are especially sensitive to how they are doing in relationship to one another. Am I better than others? Worse than others? Better off? Worse off?

- *Evaluation.* Middles are quick to make judgments about one another, and these judgments are generally based on surface characteristics: how the others dress; how they wear their hair; their physical characteristics, gender, skin color; how they speak; whether they are too emotional or too rational, and so on.

- *No collective power.* Middles feel there is no potential for collective power among them. Potential collective power lies with Tops or Bottoms, but not with them.

- *Disinterest.* Given how they feel about one another, it is not surprising that these people have little interest in being together.

- *System consequence.* Uneven treatment across groups, duplication of effort, lack of coordination, loss of potential synergies, inconsistent information coming up to Tops, and inconsistent execution of Top initiatives.

Bottom Groups Fall into GroupThink

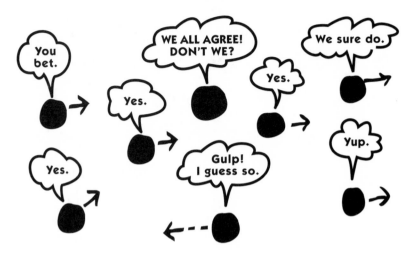

The Basic GroupThink pattern:

- A "We" mentality develops among the members of the group. Members feel closely identified with one another on the basis of a common cause or purpose or racial, ethnic, or national identity.

- Clear boundaries are drawn between the "We" and all others ("Them").

- Members feel and exert on one another a pressure to maintain unity within the group.

Common symptoms of Bottom GroupThink:

- *Inflated sense of value.* Members have a high (often inflated) sense of their own worth in comparison to "Them."

- *Differential treatment of "Them."* Since Others are seen as lesser than group members, they can be treated in ways one would not treat group members. This differential treatment ranges from relatively mild misconduct (poking fun at one's supervisor) to playing fast and loose with their rules, to breaking their laws, to defacing or destroying their property, to sabotage, to terrorism.

- *Pressure to conform.* There are strong pressures toward uniformity within the group. These are pressures that members place on themselves and on one another. Pressures to conform range from subtle (gentle jabbing) to oppressive (coercion, "tough love," reeducation).

- *Exile.* Those who deviate too far from the group norms and cannot be brought into line are exiled from the group and called "scabs" and "traitors." As an exile, one is subject to the same treatment given "Them."

- *Splintering.* Apparently irreconcilable factions develop in the group. Factions split off and treat one another as "Thems." An example is the splintering among once uniform labor, religious, political, radical, and philosophical groups.

- *Submergence.* To maintain their place in the group, some members submerge their differences; they go along with the group story line though they disagree with it. Some members hide their differences from themselves.

- *Village Idiots.* Some diverging members are kept in the group but ignored. They speak, but no one listens. It is as if they are invisible. They are treated by the group as the Village Idiots. Although this is clearly a group dysfunction, the Village Idiot becomes the "sick" member while the others remain "sane." (See 50, "Immigrant Martha has a Breakdown.")

- *System consequences.* Energy that could be devoted to pursuing a common goal—whether it is doing the work of the system or working to change the system—is wasted on internal struggle. In the pursuit of "in unity there is strength," the potential power of "in diversity there is strength" is lost.

How Do Group Members Explain These Relationship Breakdowns?

People believe that their reactions and feelings toward one another are based on real and substantial differences among them. They attribute their relationship breakdowns to the personal characteristics of the parties involved or to an unfortunate mixture of personality types within the group. There is no sense that they have simply fallen into the Dance of Blind Reflex.

He: The more I hear, the more puzzled I get. I don't wake up every morning and say, "Hey gang, I've got a good idea. Why don't we do the Dance of Blind Reflex?"

We keep thinking we're unique, making our own choices, dealing with our special situations. And then I see this. Like it's all written out in advance. It's a puzzle.

She: Only from the inside. From the outside, it's all very clear. You will see. I promise you. What seems real are merely the illusions of the system spaces people occupy.

He: How does this happen?

She: It happens because we are blind to system processes. Let me give you a summary.

38 Relationship Breakdowns in a Nutshell

She: Top, Middle, and Bottom groups are systems within the system. They are components of a single organization, yet each component struggles to survive in its own unique environment within the organization. Different environments necessitate different survival processes. However, much to our detriment, we get stuck on these survival processes and neglect other important processes. And the key factor is, we don't see any of this happening. So when relationships break down within our systems, we think it's personal. In a nutshell, it's something like this:

System	Environment	Survival Process	Overlooked Processes	Consciousness	Relationship Breakdown
Top Groups	Complexity and Accountability	Differentiation	Homogenization Integration	Mine	Turf
Middle Groups	Diffusion	Individuation	Integration	I	Alienation
Bottom Groups	Shared Vulnerability	Integration	Individuation and Differentiation	We	Group Think

He: I think I need a bit more detail.

Scene 2
From Process Blindness to Process Sight

39 Territorial Tops: Stuck on Differentiation

Put us together in a Top Space—
a space of complexity
and accountability;
a space in which together
we have designated responsibility for the system
or subsystem—
the organization,
the family,
the classroom,

the plant,
the team;
a space in which there are
many complex,
difficult,
and changing issues for us to deal with.

We *differentiate*
in order to cope
with that responsibility
and complexity:
"You handle this,
I'll handle that,
she'll handle those,
and he'll handle the other."

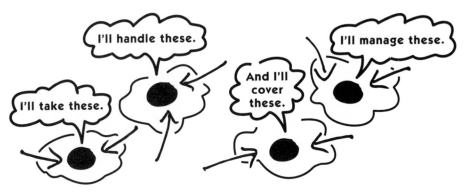

Differentiation
is imperative for us;
without it,
we would be overwhelmed,
unable to cope with all of the dangers,
unable to prospect among the opportunities.
However . . .
we soon become stuck on differentiation.

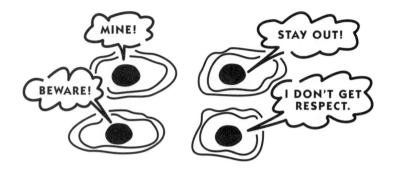

We become complex and specialized.
I elaborate my capacities to perform my functions
and shut off my capacities to perform yours.
You do the same.
We grow increasingly different from one another.

We fall into our **mine** consciousness—
This is my territory; keep out!
We fall into turf battles—
increasingly territorial,
increasingly responsible for and knowledgeable about our
own differentiations,
decreasingly responsible for and knowledgeable about the
differentiations of others and the system as a whole.
We pile up redundant resources in our separate stovepipes;
we send conflicting and confusing messages throughout the
system.
In addition to our **functional** differentiations,
we fall into **directional** differentiations—
which direction should the system as a whole take?
Expansive or conservative? Rapid growth or slow? Hierarchical
or democratic? Stability or change?

We fall into relationship problems—

not feeling respected for our contributions,

not feeling supported,

not trusting or feeling trusted.

Potential productive synergies between our areas are lost.

And when we don't see systems,

all of these feelings seem like reality to us,

the way things *really* are.

Our explanations are *personal*: you or me, an unfortunate mix

of temperaments or values or personality quirks;

or our explanations are *situational*: it's the peculiarities of the

situation we are in.

It's funny how this turned out, isn't it?

When we began,

we thought we were the perfect

executive team,

couple,

business partners.

40 The Success of a Business, the Failure of Its Partners

Until recently Charles and Edgar were partners (Tops) in a department store business. What began twenty-five years ago with a single under-stocked store, struggling to survive in a quiet neighborhood, gradually grew into a chain of five busy and successful department stores, well situated in an active, urban shopping area.

As the business grew and the partners prospered, their personal relationship deteriorated. What had begun in friendship and a shared determination to succeed evolved into a painful history of continuous and escalating conflict. And then the partnership ended.

The pattern of conflict—toward the end at least—was clear and consistent. Each player had the other neatly pegged: Edgar was the reckless expansionist, and Charles was the overly cautious conservative.

Generally, Edgar wanted to move more quickly on business matters than did Charles: expand, develop new departments, open new stores, adopt new management control systems, hire and fire personnel, switch from one buying service to another, invest large sums of money in "good buys," and so forth.

Charles, by contrast, was consistently on the side of caution: maintaining the status quo or pressing for slower and more secure development, fiscally conservative, and more patient with store managers, personnel, and vendors.

■   ■   ■

From a systems perspective, one might describe this as a healthy process. Isn't it beautiful to see how the system is differentiating, how it is exploring its possibilities? What kind of system shall we be? How shall we grow? One might even speculate that the tension between these two emerging differentiations is a healthy process—a creative tension that keeps the system from either expanding beyond its capacity to survive or sinking into zero-growth death. One might reasonably speculate that that creative tension is what accounted for the system's steady growth.

Neither Charles nor Edgar was seeing the system. To them, this was purely a struggle between personalities. And so the relationship became personalized rather than systemized, and as such, it fell into the familiar pattern of differentiation leading to "stuck on differentiation," leading to Turf Warfare, leading to polarization, leading to the dissolution of the partnership.

For Edgar, Charles was the stumbling block, the naysayer standing in the way of business progress. And for Edgar, the nay-saying went beyond business; he felt that Charles neither liked nor respected him.

He felt that he was too often dismissed, that he was working daily beside a man who doubted his intelligence, failed to respect his judgment, disliked him personally, and refused to give his ideas the full hearing they deserved. As a result, Edgar's attacks on Charles comprised more than a rational analysis of the pros and cons of particular decisions; they bore the added emotionality of one who feels unloved, not respected, and unheard.

Charles, on the other hand, felt that for years he had been living on the edge of disaster. He saw Edgar as a reckless gambler who needed to be controlled if the business were to survive. Charles feared that an unbridled Edgar would keep the business and the partnership in a perpetual state of chaos and would stretch the financial capacity of the business to the breaking point. And beyond business matters, Charles often felt menaced by Edgar's personal style. He saw Edgar as irrational and abusive. He couldn't discuss anything calmly with him. If Charles raised an objection, Edgar would shout and scream and abruptly end the conversation.

After years of turmoil marked by periodic threats of separation, Edgar bought out Charles's share of the business, and the partnership came to an end.

She: Differentiation is such a beautiful process. It's proof that the system is alive, that it is elaborating its possibilities. Of course, not all differentiations turn out to be functional. Some become blind alleys. But what's to be appreciated is the fact that they all reflect the system's attempt to survive and develop.

He: Are you saying that this whole breakdown between Charles and Edgar was systemic? They did seem to have some powerful personality differences.

She: Of course they did, but it is the systemic craziness that did them in. Systemic craziness multiplies interpersonal craziness.

He: They seemed such stereotypes: Edgar always reckless, Charles always cautious.

She: When we get stuck on differentiation, we polarize. We make one another into stereotypes.

He: That's a neat trick. How do we do it?

She: Let's assume that Charles and Edgar don't start out as stereotypes. Charles is more conservative than Edgar, but he also has an expansive side. And Edgar is more expansive than Charles, but he also has his conservative side. So now let's say an issue comes up, and there's a choice to be either conservative or expansive. What do you think Charles and Edgar will do?

He: They'll probably go with their strong side: Edgar will go expansive, and Charles will go conservative.

She: Right. And that's all they ever see of one another. They never see the other side.

He: So Edgar starts to feel that if he doesn't push for expansion, no one ever will.

She: Exactly. And that makes him very nervous, so he feels he must push harder.

He: And the same thing happens with Charles. He never sees any signs of caution from Edgar, which makes him very nervous, so he pushes harder to conserve.

She: And now we have a perfectly antagonistic set of stereotypes.

He: Beautiful on the outside, deadly on the inside.

41 Learning from Experience: A Good Second Marriage

A colleague told me about a remarkable group of Tops. "These people are like survivors of bad first marriages," he said. "What's special about them is that they learned from their mistakes and are committed to not repeating them." Each of these Tops had had, in previous positions, painful experiences with the personal and organizational consequences of Turf Warfare. And each was committed to creating something more constructive in this new organization. Their motto: Never again!

How did they do it?

They spent much time "walking in one another's shoes." They all had their own areas of responsibility, yet they arranged to spend considerable time together: regularly traveling together, sharing information, learning about one another's arenas.

They became good coaches to one another. Each of them knew full well what it was to be a Burdened Top, and they were experts at spotting one another's dysfunctional responses to overload. "When we see one of us racing off the cliff, someone's there to slow them down."

They invested a good deal of authority in their Middles, which opened up valuable space for the Tops to deal with issues that would otherwise have been neglected or treated in less depth.

They opened their territories to one another. It was not unusual for them to come together to focus their energies on what was generally considered someone's functional responsibility. For example, when it was time to rethink the organization-wide incentive plan, it became a collaborative project for the Top team, rather than "Human Resources' business."

My colleague said: "It works. They are a team. Ideas germinate in that group and blossom out. They look forward to working with one another."

He: So maybe that's what it takes—one bad experience—to learn.

She: Unfortunately, not everyone learns from experience. If you're committed to believing that the last bad experience was due to an unfortunate mix of personalities—

He: Or to "philosophical differences"—

She: Then there's nothing learned, and you're ready to start the same cycle over again.

42 Help! No Recovering Top Groups Sighted

I having been searching my memory for examples of Recovering Top groups—that is, Top Groups that, having fallen into Turf Warfare, have been able to recover and find their way back into partnership. No luck. What keeps coming back to me are example after example of permanent failures in Top systems: Turf Warfare, breakdown, dissolution of the system. Once it's broken, it stays broken. (Even as I was writing this, the morning newspaper told of still another partnership that began with promise and ended in breakdown. That time it was two restauranteurs; the reason, the ever-popular "philosophical differences.")

My own life has been touched again and again by disastrous Top group experiences. My father and uncle became business partners and ended their lives not speaking to one another. The same fate befell my two brothers. I went into business with my dearest friend, and not only did the business dissolve, but so did our friendship. Add to this the collapse of my first marriage, and you have quite a record of failure in the Top system. This qualifies me as an expert (and that's an understatement) on the pitfalls of the Top system. I do believe, however, that this difficulty in identifying successful cases in which a Top group, once having fallen into Turf Warfare, is able to break through into partnership is more than a personal or familial matter.

Whenever a systemic breakdown occurs—whether in Top, Middle, or Bottom systems—the breakdown is most generally experienced as personal. The fault, you feel, must lie with you or with me or with our particular mix of characteristics. And the explanations feel solid—the way things *really* are. And if you were to suggest that these breakdowns are not personal but systemic, you should expect resistance—not relief. That is true of all three systems, but there is an added element in the Top system that contributes an emotional bite to the breakdown. For the most part, we do not choose our membership in Middle and Bottom systems; we find ourselves there. This is not the case with Top systems; we *choose* our membership in these. We choose our marriage and business partners: Top Executive teams are assembled on the basis of exceptional mixtures of talents; friends and relatives feel that their history and love for one another will ensure business success. And it is under these conditions of choice that failure is particularly painful. We begin with such promise, but the more powerful the promise, the greater the sense of loss, disappointment, and betrayal. It's one thing to treat strangers this way, but to treat friends and relations this way is unforgivable. The separations become irreconcilable. It would take a terrible shaking of the dance to effect a transformation.

So I am still waiting for that first recovery in the Top system. I'm waiting for Edgar to suddenly see the light and slap himself on the forehead. "My God!" he'll say. "I see it now. There's nothing wrong with Charles . . . or with me. What we have here is a failure in differentiation. Charles and I are OK. The problem is not with us, and the solution is not to fix us. The solution is to see how, together, we can master this space of complexity and responsibility."

I'm still waiting.

He: Short of waiting, isn't there something more productive we can do?

She: We can warn people. Warning: You are entering the Top system!

43 Advice for the Top Team

This is a warning to all Top Teams:

Newly married couples,
Newly formed executive teams,
New business partners.

Caution: You are entering the Top Space—
a space of *complexity*
and *accountability*.

Your life is about to change.

Personally, your mood is likely to shift
from light to heavy—
from feeling responsible for yourself
to feeling responsible for others
(sometimes very many others),
from feeling relatively carefree
to chronic worrying.

Your relationships with your partner(s)
are subject to strain.
You may be entering this partnership
convinced that you are the perfect team.
Those feelings are subject to dramatic change.

Do not believe that you are immune to these processes.
You and your partner(s) may be very special people,
but these processes are not about people,
they are about living in the Top Space.
Strange things can happen to the nicest people
when they get together in the Top Space.

Pursue the following steps, and not only will you save your relationship from deteriorating, you will deepen and strengthen it well beyond its current condition.

Your challenge in the Top Space is to become adept at managing complexity and accountability without becoming overwhelmed. The general strategies are:

Keep it simple.

Differentiate with zest.

Homogenize with zest.

1. *Keep it simple.* Watch out for the tendency to take on responsibility for everything. The Top Space is complex enough without your assuming responsibility for things others could be handling. A

major aspect of your Top responsibility is the ability to create responsibility in others.

2. *Differentiate with zest.* This is not likely to be a problem. It will happen. Circumstances will force differentiation on you. Your situation is complex; to cope with that complexity and not be overwhelmed by it, you and your partners will find yourselves differentiating—certain partners taking on primary responsibility for certain functions, others taking on primary responsibility for other functions.

   Pursue your differentiations with zest; become expert in them and perform them diligently and elegantly.

3. *Homogenize with zest.* This is what will make or break your partnership. Homogenization does not come naturally in the Top Space. You need to work at it. Here your goal is to maintain and strengthen your *commonality*. The following are some homogenizing strategies:

   - *Vision.* Come to agreement on a common vision for this system (family, organization, partnership). What are your fondest wishes for what it will become? This will become an important foundation to revisit when there is tension among the partners.

   - *Shared information.* Regularly share information with one another regarding the events, issues, difficulties, and choices in your respective areas of responsibility.

   - *Mutual coaching.* Create coaching relationships with one another such that each of you, as coach to the other(s), becomes fully committed to the other's success as well as to your own. Mutual coaching is likely to be the most powerful process for maintaining and strengthening both your partnership and the system for which you have joint responsibility.

   - *Interchangeability.* Create regular opportunities to walk in the others' shoes, experiencing their worlds and the issues they are dealing with.

   - *Joint task forces.* Find opportunities to partner with one another when new issues arise that fall outside your areas of responsibility.

He: Homogenization! Generally we think of that as a bad thing, like all the world is starting to look the same.

She: Keep your eye on homogenization. It is a critical process for system success. And it is the one most frequently overlooked.

Wherever there is differentiation—

the elaboration of our differences—

special attention needs to be given to

homogenization,

developing and maintaining our commonality.

Top systems exist in environments of

complexity and accountability;

to survive in those environments,

Top systems differentiate.

Then they get stuck on differentiation,

and that's when Turf Warfare sets in.

44 Alienated Middles: Stuck on Individuation

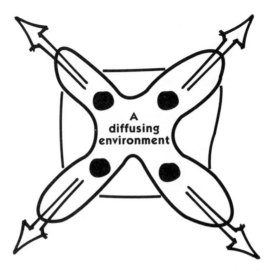

Put us together
in a *diffusing* space—
a space that draws us *away* from one another,
out toward other compelling
individuals,
groups,
activities—
and we become a collection of independent "I's."

Even when together
in our groups or neighborhoods,
we fall into our *I* consciousness
in which our separateness predominates.
We experience ourselves as unique (which we may be),
having little in common with one another (which is not true),

feeling competitive with one another,

being evaluative of one another.

It is crystal clear to us:

This is no group,

and there is no collective power in here.

Feeling as we do about one another,

we stay apart;

staying apart reinforces our *I* consciousness

("Why would I spend more time with such people?"),

which reinforces our staying apart,

which completes the cycle of alienation.

And when we don't see systems,

all of these perceptions, evaluations, and feelings

are reality to us—

the way things *really* are.

Alienation is the illusion of the Middle Space.

45 Alienation Among the Middles

When we don't see systems,
we are at their mercy.

Of the three classes in the Power Lab, the Middles are invariably the most disintegrated. The Middles share a common house and a common title (Middles or Managers), they eat at a common table, they sometimes meet together, but they remain a collection of autonomous individuals. The Middle class rarely has a position or platform of its own in the society; it functions between the conflicting positions and platforms of the Elite and the Immigrants. Individual Middles are drawn toward either (1) aligning themselves with the Elite or the Immigrants or (2) remaining torn between the two. The Middle house is usually an uninviting place; it is clear that nothing of much significance happens there.

In the Middle Space, even when we are together, it is as if our backs are turned to one another.

Consider the following:

The Middles are having dinner "together"; that is, they are sharing the same table.

Stan approaches. He has been trying to get the attention of his associate Middles, but he is having little success.

"I need to talk with you," he says. There is no response. Each of Stan's associates is busily at work on his or her own business.

Court Officer Carla is shuffling through a stack of proposals she has received from the Immigrants. She is under pressure from her boss to get these proposals sorted out. Carla is also disconcerted by the fact that her rent is due and she hasn't yet been paid.

"They're giving me a hard time," says Stan, referring to the Immigrants. Still no response.

Kerry is working diligently on a financial report for her boss. She is responsible for the store and supplies, and her boss has been complaining about the poor quality of her reporting. She hardly glances up as Stan speaks.

Bill, who is responsible for employment, is preparing a work status report. His boss just came by the table, complaining that the report was past due and asking that it be ready in thirty minutes.

"The Immigrants are giving me a hard time," says Stan, still standing by the table. That catches Court Officer Carla's attention. "Are there any infractions?" she asks. As Court Officer, infractions are Carla's business. She shows little interest in whatever other problems Stan might be having. "I'll assume everything's legal unless you tell me otherwise," she says as she returns to perusing her stack of proposals.

Stan stands awkwardly at the table. Finally, he speaks (to no one in particular): "Should I just start talking?"

Might as well, Stan.

He: I've had many such "conversations" with my Middle peers.

She: You are not alone. Fear and loathing in the Middle Space is not exactly an uncommon condition—members feeling unique, having little in common, feeling competitive and evaluative, believing that there's no collective power in this Middle group, there's no point in being together.

He: As you run down that list, I find myself thinking as much about my neighbors as about my organizational peers. We're also competitive, evaluative, unique. We're focused on who does what with their lawn or pool or deck. You know what I mean: one trying to outdo the other.

She: Much of our lives is spent in this diffusing space. We are pulled apart from one another and fall into the illusion of alienation.

Exercise

Take yourself to an airport or train or bus station—
perfect diffusing spaces.
Most of the folks you see don't belong here;
they are heading somewhere else.
Find a bench where you can sit and watch all the people
passing by.
And watch yourself watching them:
This one is attractive, and this one is not;
this one does funny things with his hair, and this one dresses
strangely;
this one is too emotional, and that one talks too loudly.
An unending stream of evaluations.

He: I don't have to go to the train station to have that experience. Just about any weekly staff meeting will do. What a bunch of alienated misfits we are.

She: Yes, but are you prepared to give that up?

He: I don't understand.

She: Are you prepared to face the possibility that that collection of misfits could become a powerful system? That you could come to like and respect one another? That you could become a powerful and effective force in your organization? That you could become a useful support system for one another? That your Tops would really value you as a team? That your Workers would see all of you as providing effective and coordinated leadership? Are you prepared to face that possibility?

He: You've got to be kidding.

She: Are you prepared to face the fact that I'm not kidding?

46 Can Alienated Middles Become a Powerful System?

He: Is there anything Middles can do so that they're not alienated?

She: Yes, but first you have to learn to distrust your experience.

He: Distrust my experience?

She: Aha! I hear the sound of the old dance shaking. When you are in the Middle Space, it all seems so real to you. It really is clear that you have little in common with the others, that there's no collective power in here, that you're not comfortable with one another, and so on. This is the evidence of your senses. So why would you even consider becoming an integrated "We" with this collection of misfits?

So the first step is to recognize that these very solid feelings and evaluations you have may not be the *cause* of your alienation from one another. More likely, they are the *result* of that alienation.

He: Come again?

She: You are in the grips of a vicious cycle. Because your world pulls you apart from one another, you fall into the "I" mentality:

We're each unique

We have little in common

We're competitive

We're evaluative of one another

And there's no collective power among us.

And being in the "I" mentality reinforces staying apart.

Why would I get together with people when we are unique, have little in common? . . . and on and on it goes.

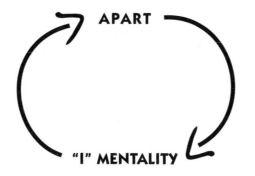

You think that the reason you don't integrate with one another is because of how you feel about one another. ("Why would I want to integrate with these people?") In fact, it's just the other way around. You feel the way you do about one another because you don't integrate. And if you did integrate, you would feel very differently about one another.

■ ■ ■

If this seems too big a pill to swallow, consider the following: We have conducted many hundreds of organization exercises over the past thirty-five years. In each exercise, people are randomly assigned to Top, Middle, or Bottom groups. At some point we ask people to describe their relationships with their group members. The comparison of the Middle and Bottom group experiences is particularly striking. With great regularity, Bottoms speak very positively about their groups, using such terms as *teamwork, sharing, supportive, high energy.* As a group, Bottoms say, "We could do the job if only *they* gave us clear direction . . . gave us the resources to do the job . . . got out of our way . . ." and so on. With equal regularity, Middles describe themselves as a nongroup. It is particularly interesting to hear Middles describe their groups very positively, only to find out that the groups they are referring to are their *Worker* groups—since the notion of Middles as a group is too ludicrous to even consider. With Middles, it is only a question of the degree of alienation among them—from simply having nothing to do with one another to extreme competitiveness, undermining of one another, and interpersonal tension.

So explanations of Middle alienation in terms of companies' hiring practices, social Darwinism, or genetic disposition simply won't do. It is clear that had those Middles been put together in Bottom groups, there is every likelihood they would have described themselves in terms of teamwork, sharing, support, "We," and so forth. This is precisely what this systemic lens is all about.

47 Mutant Middle Groups

"Middle group" is generally an oxymoron:

If they're Middles, they're not a group;

and if they're a group, they're not Middles.

Generally, that's the case.

Generally . . . but not always.

It is the exception that points the way to possibility.

Some years ago, I was delivering a lecture on Middle power and powerlessness. The lecture was, for the most part, pure theory: *Here is the nature of Middle Space. Here is what happens to a collection of sane, healthy, competent people when you put them together in that space. Here is how they disintegrate personally and collectively. And here is what you must do if you want to create powerful teams of Middles.*

The theory was solid; it was backed by years of observations of Middle groups in our organizational and community simulations. And although at the time I was not much involved in "real world" organizations, I began to hear from folks who were, that these were precisely the dynamics they were living with.

The First Mutation

One story I told had to do with the first Middle group mutation I had experienced. It came about during a multiple-day workshop. Each day there was an organization exercise involving Tops, Middles, Bottoms, and Customers. On the first day, the traditional Middle group dance unfolded: the disintegration of Middles individually and collectively. On the second day, a new group of Middles approached the exercise, determined to show everyone what *real* Middles could do. The results were the same: Personal and collective disintegration. It was on the third day that the mutation appeared.

The Simple Agreement

The members of this third group of Middles made a simple agreement with one another: They were to meet at the beginning and middle of each work period—just Middles, no Tops—to share information, identify issues they all needed to work on, and stay coordinated. The agreement was to meet *no matter what competing pressures there were.* For it had been made clear that in this diffusing Middle Space, there were always competing pressures: Your work group needs to see you now, or the Tops need to meet with you, or the Customers need you. The Middles would make it clear to others that these Middle meetings were commitments and were critical to organizational health and customer service, let alone their own sanity.

As is the case with all transformations, there was resistance. No one appreciated being put off. *Why do Middles have to meet?* The Middles persisted, and the transformation was total. In the end, Tops and

Bottoms agreed that the Middles played the central role in the organization's success. Both saw the Middles as a strong and effective unit. The Middles seemed to be in synch with one another; they did not experience disintegration personally or collectively. They felt like a team. A remarkable outcome for Middles! They had alleviated the burdens of Tops, provided strong, informed, and consistent leadership for their Workers, and developed solid relationships with one another. And all of this by simply making *and sticking to* the commitment to meet regularly with one another.

The First Practical Application

Bob DuBrul, a consultant, was in the audience that day. Bob and I were not to meet face to face for several years, but when we did, he told me the following story. My lecture had set him thinking: This familiar, disintegrated Middle group pattern seems to fit many of his client systems. Were powerful Middle teams possible? Could this commitment to regular integration work? Bob was hesitant. He knew there would be considerable resistance from the Middles themselves. The usual litany: *Why should we get together? We have little in common. We don't get along with one another. There's no power in here.* So Bob held off.

That summer, his daughter, Tresa Amrani, became director of counselors—Top—at a summer camp. In one of their conversations, she let on how burdened she was by the complexities and responsibilities of the job. There were issues she needed to deal with from her counselors, from the camp directors, from activities directors, from parents, and more. She was unable to keep up. She was particularly troubled by the decisions her counselors were bringing to her—matters she felt they, themselves, were perfectly capable of handling. There were other issues among the counselors: competition, personal squabbles, lack of coordination, inconsistency.

Tresa's situation brought back to Bob the picture of Middle group disintegration and the possibilities of Middle power. They discussed the situation, and Tresa launched the first (to my knowledge) "real world" application of the theory. She created the counselors as a self-regulating Middle team. Their charge was to work collectively to manage the bulk of the day-to-day operations of the camp. They met regularly—without Tresa—to do whatever business had to be done.

The Sound of Two Dances Shaking

There was resistance, as one would predict. There were two dances being disrupted here: the Top/Bottom dance between Tresa and the counselors and the Alienated Middle dance going on among the counselors. There were many issues that needed to be dealt with (some of which we'll discuss shortly), but the experiment was a resounding success. The counselors basically ran the operation, and Tresa was freed up to do her Top business.

Again, it was some years later that Bob and I met and Bob told me this story and others about his rich experiences working with Middle integration. Tresa's experience had given Bob the confidence to begin to work with Middle integration in his own practice.

The shift doesn't always work, particularly if Middles withhold themselves from *active* integration; just sitting together waiting for the miracle to come, it never *will* come (see the following section, "'It' Never Works"). But when the shift does work, the transformation of the Middle Space is nearly miraculous. Bob described one plant at which the plant manager claimed his integrating Middle team now runs the bulk of the day-to-day operations of the plant. This plant manager's boss said that, of all the plant managers, this one was the only one having fun. Much of the plant manager's burden was relieved by the integrating Middle team. Workers have great respect for these Middles: they see them as coordinated and as providing strong, consistent, and informed leadership. In time, the compensation structure was modified to fit the new reality, such that the Middles were paid 50 percent for how well they individually managed their units and 50 percent for how well they collectively integrated the whole.

"We Need Your Leadership"

There is one other piece to this story. One day Bob was called in by the Top of an integrating Middle group. One of the Middles had come to the Top, saying that the Middles were stuck on a particular issue. "We need your leadership," said the Middle. (What Top can resist that call?) The Top asked Bob what he thought he should do. Bob said he'd think about it. Bob called Tresa.

"Exactly the same thing happened to me," she said. "One of the counselors said they couldn't work out some issue and they needed me."

"What did you do?"

"I told them they could work it out."

"And did they?"

"They did."

So Bob went back to the Top and advised him to stay out of the issue and encourage the Middles to resolve it themselves, which they did. And the lesson for Bob and for all of us is this: *It is precisely in having to face and deal with the most difficult issues that the possibility of Middle power lies.*

"It" Never Works

Some experiments with Middle integration have worked, some haven't. One Middle once said to me, "We tried integration, and it didn't work. Nothing happened." Well, it's true: Nothing ever happens. I imagined these Middles sitting silently in a room, tapping their feet, glancing at their watches, waiting for some miracle to strike. It doesn't happen that way. For Middle integration to happen, the players must disrupt two comfortably uncomfortable dances: the Top/Bottom dance and the Alienated Middles dance. There are myriad opportunities for resistance. Are Middles ready to give up their Bottomness and become Top? Is Top ready to allow Middles to be Top? Are Middles (all of them) ready to give up their alienation from one another? There are many people and many opportunities to say "No." And "No" can end the process.

As usual, it comes down to how one responds to "No." Is it the end of the process? Are Middles, even in the face of resistance from Top, willing to persist in their efforts to integrate? Is Top, even in the face of resistance from Middles, willing to persist in creating an integrating Middle team? Are Middles, even in the face of resistance from one another, willing to persist in overcoming their alienation? Is "No" the end of the process? Or is it the sound of two dances shaking?

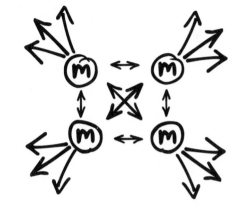

When Middles Are Dis-Integrated	**When Middles Integrate**
They are alone, unsupported, not part of Top or Bottom, not even connected with one another.	They have a supportive peer group.
They are uninformed, easily surprised.	Through regular sharing of information, they are highly informed.
They are focused on their group's needs.	They are focused on what their group needs and on what the system needs.
They are seen by Workers as weak, uninformed, fractionated.	They are seen as having the goods, being consistent, and providing strong leadership.
Uneven practices among Middles are seen as inconsistent, unfair.	They are seen as fair, consistent, coordinated.
Top is responsible for system integration.	Middles handle system integration. Top is freed up to do Top business.
Top complaints: Middles aren't entrepreneurial enough. Can't get initiatives down through the Middles. Don't get consistent information from Middles.	Middles identify and work on needed initiatives. Top puts initiatives into the Middle group; Middles work them around and then move them into the system consistently and quickly. Middles provide consistent information.

48 How to Create Powerful Middle Teams

In Middle groups
special attention needs to be paid to integration.
In the diffusing environment,
integration will not happen naturally;
it has to be worked at
rigorously.

1. Believe that it's possible.

2. Create a compelling *mission* for yourselves, a *collective* mission that is different from the *individual* missions you have for the groups you lead, manage, or coach. *What can this Middle Team do that has never been done before? What can we do better than it has ever been done before?* The more compelling your mission, the stronger the glue that will hold you together.

3. Get past the myths of alienation. Find out who you are and what really matters to you. Learn about one another's personal interests, projects, passions, or missions.

4. Support one another in pursuing the group's mission.

5. Support one another in pursuing your personal projects.

6. Create regular meetings and processes for sharing information, supporting one another, coaching one another.

7. Break bread together.

8. Treat these meetings and processes as sacred commitments.

9. Be ready to be surprised.

10. Remember: Alienation is an illusion of the Middle Space.

He: That's a great idea.

She: But?

He: But it wouldn't work with my group.

She: Why?

He: Why? Because we're unique, we have little in common, we don't get along with one another, we're competitive, there's no point in our getting together, there's no collective power in here . . .

I'm kidding. I'm kidding.

She: I hope so.

Top systems exist in environments of

complexity and accountability;

to survive in those environments,

Top systems differentiate.

Then they get stuck on differentiation,

and that's when Turf Warfare sets in.

Middle systems exist in

diffusing environments;

to survive in those environments,

Middle systems individuate.

Then they get stuck on individuation,

and that's when Alienation sets in.

49 Bottom GroupThink: Stuck on Integration

From "I" to "We"

Put us together

in a space of *vulnerability*,

a space in which some important aspect of our existence

feels threatened—

our livelihood,

our neighborhood,

our way of life,

our nation,

our religion or ethnic group—

and we fall into our *"We"* consciousness

in which our connectedness to one another predominates,

integrated components of some larger "It"—

the Group,

the Neighborhood,

the Nation

the Religion

the Race.

The "We" Is More Powerful Than the "I"
We become one with that entity,
enhanced in it—
stronger,
timeless,
nobler,
heroic.
There is something special about
our Neighborhood,
we Workers,
our Nation,
our Religion,
our Social Class,
even our Sports Team.

"We" Against "Them"
There is no "We" without some "Them"—
Management,
another Neighborhood,
another Nation,
another Ethnic Group,
another Religion.
The enhancement of the "We"
allows us to do damage to others.
When we are stuck in the "We,"
we can abuse these others,
hurt them,
oppress them,
and even destroy them
with little shame or guilt,
because in our "We"-ness

it is crystal clear that "They"
are different,
lesser
than the "We."

Trouble Within the "We"
When we are stuck in "We,"
there is no room for the Ones Who Disagree.
When we are stuck in "We,"
the Ones Who Disagree become dangerous
to others
and to themselves.
When the Ones Who Disagree slip too far from the "We,"
the "We" grow anxious—
We must bring the Ones Who Disagree back into line—
love them,
educate them,
coerce them into line.
And if we can't bring them into line,
we must shun them,
confine them,
jail them,
exile them,
or eliminate them.

And when the Ones Who Disagree slip too far from the
"We,"
the "Ones" grow anxious too.
The "Ones" need the "We,"
so the "Ones" may hide their disagreement from the "We";
go along with the "We"

even though they disagree;
go along
with false zest
or in apathy
and shame.

And sometimes
the Ones Who Disagree hide their disagreement even from
themselves
and become mysteriously ill.

■   ■   ■

Which brings us to Martha's mysterious breakdown.

50 Immigrant Martha Has a Breakdown

The following case comes from an early Power Lab. It is one of many that helped us see into life within the "We."

A negotiating session is in progress. Involved are representatives of the Elite, the Managers (Middles), and the Immigrants. The society has been fractionated for days, and it has been a struggle to bring all parties to the table. But here they are at last. A specific set of agenda items has been agreed to. Members of the society not directly involved in the negotiations are invited to observe the process but are prohibited from interfering with it.

Immigrant Martha is standing behind the negotiating table observing. The complete agenda has been laid out, and work on the first few items is proceeding. The process is rational and orderly: Items are presented and clarified, offers are made, caucuses are held, counter-proposals are offered. All in all, a very different climate exists from that which characterized previous interchanges among Elite, Managers, and Immigrants.

Martha becomes distraught. Fighting back tears, she runs from the room. The Negotiators pause momentarily, then continue with their work. A few minutes later, Martha returns. It is obvious that she has been crying, and she is trembling now. She interrupts the negotiating process, sobbing while fighting to get the words out: "We (Immigrants) are in a degraded position . . . We are asking for minimal things . . ." She sobs, catches her breath, and musters the strength to continue. Then, her body trembling, her face flushed in rage, she shouts: "I . . . AM . . . SICK . . . AND . . . TIRED . . . OF . . . IT. THAT IS WHERE I AM . . . I CANNOT TAKE THIS ANYMORE . . . I CANNOT WATCH THIS ANYMORE . . . IT IS TOO DEGRADING . . . I AM LEAVING." She storms out of the room, and the negotiating process stops.

Gerri, an Immigrant Negotiator, says, "This is beyond our capacity to handle. It is beyond the scope of the game. Martha is an unstable person. She's fragile and she's going to need competent psychological help." Other Immigrants nod their heads in agreement. Martha has been shaky of late: withdrawn, crying, displaying bursts of anger not only at the Elite and Managers but, more commonly, at her associate Workers. "She's an unstable person," says Gerri, "and she needs professional help."

■   ■   ■

When we don't see systems, we see individual personalities. Our explanations are personal, and our solutions are personal. Fix the individual. In this case, fix Martha. When we see systems, quite another world opens up to us. What we have here is not a personal problem but a social disease—a disorder of the "We." What we have here is a failure in differentiation.

Within the "We," two competing forces come into play. There are powerful pressures to remain a uniform "We," for in this solidarity lies strength. However, working against that uniformity are the variations that inevitably develop within the "We."

Given enough time, *in all Bottom groups* a directional differentiation develops regarding the best way to handle our vulnerability to "Them"—should "We" be tough or soft with "Them"? Should "We" be polite or confrontational? Should "We" enter into negotiations or take direct action? The form and intensity of the differences vary from system to system. (In one setting, "tough" might mean "Let's complain" and "soft" might mean "Let's not complain"; much further along the continuum, "soft" might mean "Let's not kill women and children.") Whatever the form and intensity, the directional differentiation occurs with great predictability, whether in Worker groups, in the organization, in oppressed groups in society, or in revolutionary groups.

In its vulnerability, the system—unable to tolerate the internal pressure caused by differentiation—resolves this tension in any number of ways, each of which serves to maintain the integrity of the "We":

- By coercing dissenters into line

- By exiling dissenters

- By jailing dissenters

- By executing dissenters

- By declaring dissenters insane

- By fractionating into separate (and usually mutually antagonistic) "We's"

    And sometimes

- By denying the existence of difference

When that happens, dissenters simply become invisible. Their suggestions are ignored; they are treated as eccentrics; they speak but no one listens. They become the Village Idiots, "crazy" while the rest of the village remains "sane." This was the fate of Immigrant Martha.

A Systemic Cure

Martha did not get her personal fix. She remained apathetic, listless, and depressed throughout the remainder of the society's life. However, she did get her cure, which turned out to have ramifications beyond Martha.

In my role as societal Anthropologist, I happened to have compiled a list of "Key Immigrant Decisions." Throughout the life of the society, issues arose requiring decisions by the Immigrants: Do we go this way or that? The choices were always on the order of: Do we take a hard or soft line with "Them"? Do we go along or resist, cooperate or fight?

Because it was a highly integrated system, no individual decisions were made. The Immigrants would caucus, discuss the issue, and come up with the group decision.

Their issues included the following:

- Do we accept their wage hike proposal?

- Do we participate in their community improvement process?

- Should Gerri leave the group and accept a promotion into Middle Management?

- Do we show up for court?

- Do we agree to participate in the negotiation process?

Now the community experience was over, and we were debriefing it. We had reviewed the Elite experience and the Manager experience, and now the Immigrants were at the front of the room—seven happy people and one depressed Martha. We spent some time talking about various aspects of the Immigrant experience. Martha was uncommunicative throughout.

Then I brought out my list of key decisions. We reviewed the decisions sequentially. I asked people to recall, as best they could, what their individual positions had been on each decision. I asked them to estimate the intensity of their feelings by using a ten-point rating system: If they felt extremely strongly in a given direction, they would score themselves 10/0; if they mildly favored one direction over the other, they might score themselves 6/4; and so forth.

We proceeded decision by decision, reviewing each issue, having people make their judgments privately, and then having them enter their judgments on a newsprint chart. This was a laborious process, and I was not at all confident that it would lead anywhere.

The data for the first decision are presented in the following table. Martha and Tim were 10/0 for resistance; all other group members were also for resistance, but with lesser intensity. The data for subsequent decisions repeated this pattern.

Decision 1

	Martha	Tim	Roger	Gerri	Bob	Nancy	Hank	Andy
Resist	10	10	6	6	8	8	7	7
Cooperate	0	0	4	4	2	2	3	3

Then on Decision 7 ("Should we enter into negotiations with the Elite?"), the pattern shifted dramatically:

Decision 7

	Martha	Tim	Roger	Gerri	Bob	Nancy	Hank	Andy
Resist	10	5	4	2	5	4	4	2
Cooperate	0	5	6	8	5	6	6	8

At this point, we talked about the data. Immigrants were struck by their early pattern of resistance: although they were in agreement about resisting, there were large differences in the intensity of feeling among them. They were also struck by the solidarity of Martha's and Tim's 10/0 responses, which brought back memories of Martha's early enthusiasm, involvement, and leadership in the group.

Then we talked about Decision 7, and Martha became quite engaged at this point. *It became clear that Martha's resistance was always of a different order than that of her associate Immigrants.* For her, the goal was radical systems change: the creation of an egalitarian society in which there were no Elite, Managers, and Immigrants—only citizens, with no distinctions in housing, work, pay, and so forth. For other Immigrants, the issue had more to do with involvement in decisions affecting their lives. They were perfectly willing to accept the three-class societal structure so long as their participation in decision making was ensured. So when the decision was made to enter into direct negotiations with the Elite on specific issues of labor, housing, pricing, and so on but to accept the basic societal structure, the split between Martha and the others became apparent. For the other Immigrants, this was a win—the beginning of their participative society—but for Martha, it was total capitulation.

I then posed a hypothetical decision point, one that had not occurred previously. This was Decision 8: Once the negotiations are under way, should we continue or break off? The data were as follows:

Decision 8

	Martha	Tim	Roger	Gerri	Bob	Nancy	Hank	Andy
Resist	10	0	0	0	0	0	0	0
Cooperate	0	10	10	10	10	10	10	10

Now the split was complete: Martha was ignored, her complaints were treated as misguided and irrelevant, her actions and emotions were viewed as eccentric. Whenever she spoke, there was little or no response. The "We" maintained its integrity—"We're all right—except for this Village Idiot."

A Mutant Moment: Seeing the System

There was an explosion of energy in the room. Martha's depression was gone; she was her old voluble, enthusiastic self. Nothing about the societal outcome had changed: Martha had still lost; the Immigrants had not totally transformed the system as she had hoped. All that had happened was "seeing." But what a difference "seeing" made for Martha and the other Immigrants! This was a "seeing" not about a person but about a system—about the processes of the whole and how these processes affected the experiences of all members. And this was not just about Martha. Something happened in the room that I still do not fully understand and can only speculate about.

The explosion of energy was not limited to the Immigrants. The Elite and Managers had been observing this process for over two hours, and when the light went on for Martha and the Immigrants, it also went on for everyone in the room. People erupted into spontaneous applause. Conversations broke out that lasted deep into the night. *This was one of those rarest of human moments—a "Mutant Moment" that illuminates a new possibility in which each of us "swimmers" see the Swim itself and how the nature of the Swim has shaped our consciousness. In that moment of "seeing," we were fully conscious and free. It is such rare moments of system seeing that heighten our more common condition of system blindness.*[1]

At one point in the conversation, Gerri, who had been Martha's most virulent adversary, said: "It could have been me."

"How do you mean?"

"Say I was the one who thought we should negotiate and everyone else said 'No.' I could easily have become the Village Idiot."

Exactly.

Who among us is incapable of seeing these dynamics of the "We"? When the "We" is for war and the One Who Disagrees is for peace? Or the other way around? When the "We" has one view of appropriate sexuality and the One Who Disagrees has another? When the "We" has one view of appropriate behavior or manner or dress and the Ones Who Disagree have other views?

■　　■　　■

He: It seems to me I've seen these same things happen in Top groups.

She: That's right. The determining factor is not where you are in the hierarchy, but what the environmental conditions of your system are. In this case, the environment is one of shared vulnerability; that is, the feeling that something precious to your group is threatened: its belief system or its way of life or its very survival.

He: So Top Executives who are feeling under attack from labor or from aggressive governmental investigations also get triggered into the "We," even though they're Tops. And they might have their Village Idiots who disagree with the "We."

She: Exactly. And when the Dominant group in society feels challenged by the Others, the Dominants get triggered into the "We."

He: So then it's "We" against "We."

She: Yes, and let me make this a bit more complex for you. Say there you are walking down the street when suddenly coming toward you is an odd-looking sight: a barefoot person with spiked rows of hair alternating orange and purple, one ring in the nose, and six tinier rings penetrating her eyebrows. Your reaction?

He: I might laugh . . . or be shocked.

She: Maybe repulsed?

He: Maybe repulsed.

She: Because?

He: I think I see what you're getting at. I laugh or am shocked or repulsed because that's not the way "We" dress.

She: Exactly. And "We" don't see ourselves as conforming. "We" see ourselves as just living.

There was one other consideration in the Martha case. Were those two Bottom group orientations really incompatible? Was it true that the group's choice was to pursue one or the other—either Martha's vision of total system transformation or the other members' more moderate aspirations for greater involvement and participation? It is a common illusion of the Bottom Space that divergences cannot be tolerated, that they will destroy the "We." ("In unity there is strength.") But it is possible that there is another kind of strength, one that comes from the realization that many such divergences are, in fact, creatively compatible; that when we work together in partnership, divergences can yield outcomes richer and more widely satisfying than those resulting from the pursuit of one or the other.

51 Where Is Everyone? A Mutant Bottom Group

We were in the middle of an organization exercise. There were twelve Bottom groups with five or six Workers in each. I was standing in the middle of the ballroom watching the action unfold when my eye was drawn to one particular Bottom group. *There was only one person sitting at this table.* I watched to see if the others had taken a break and would return shortly. But no, the table remained empty except for this one person. What had happened here? Had the others quit the organization? Worse still, I wondered if they had dropped out of the exercise. I was feeling bad for this sole survivor. I walked over full of sympathy for his isolated condition, only to find that something quite different was going on here—something I had never seen before.

He told me that the group was facing several issues. They hadn't been paid for several days, as their manager had been tied up in meetings with Tops; there had been talk about potential bonuses for Workers; there were Customers complaining about not having their projects worked on; and there was interest in having a coffee break.

I wish I had been privy to the conversation among the group members, but I was not. The outcome, however, was the breakthrough idea that *all of these issues could be addressed simultaneously.*

"Our Customer project is simple enough for me to handle alone," said the lone Worker, "and the others are out there seeing what they can do." Two members were hunting up disgruntled Customers to see if they could service them. One member was searching out their Manager to see if progress could be made both on collecting their overdue salaries and on exploring bonus possibilities for taking on additional Customer projects. And one member was bringing back coffee and pastries for a "working break."

This group had astounding success. They completed three projects—Customers were pleased, Workers got their pay along with healthy bonuses, and the group enjoyed their working break—and they had an incredible sense of teamwork and accomplishment.

This is not how it normally goes in the Bottom group. Differentiation does not come naturally, even when differentiation is what is required for the system to successfully cope with the dangers it faces and prospect among the opportunities in its environment. The strong pressure to remain an integrated "We" works against needed differentiation.

More often you would find Bottom groups focused on either the work or the working conditions, but not on both. There would be the "good Worker groups" just pouring their energies into the work ("We didn't even think about money," they would say righteously), only to find themselves unfairly underpaid at the end. Or there would be the "troublemaking Worker groups," so focused on issues of pay and working conditions that little or no work gets done.

And within these groups there would be tensions. Within the "good Worker group" there would be the submerged, disgruntled member who feels the group is being taken advantage of. Within the "trouble-makers" there would be the submerged, disgruntled member who feels the group should be cooperating.

But here we had a breakthrough: we can work and we can make sure we are being treated fairly; we can produce and we can protect ourselves. From the outside this seems so obvious; on the inside, however, when we are in the grips of "We"-ness (when we are stuck on integration), we are often blind to the obvious.

He: I wonder how many family vacations go badly because everyone feels everything has to be done together. Stuck in the "We."

She: I wonder.

52 Power Is Managing Differentiation

Once you see systems as wholes, you also begin to see power differently. From a systems perspective, power has little to do with strength or command presence or toughness or the position you hold or even the size and quality of the resources you control. *System Power is the ability to influence system processes*—to act in ways that enhance the capacity of the system to survive and develop in its environment, to cope with the dangers facing it and prospect among the opportunities. (Unless, of course, your goal is to destroy the system; then power becomes the ability to act in ways that reduce the system's capacity to survive and develop.) But to influence system processes, you must first see them.

Mutant Bottom Groups

Fritz Steele was my colleague in the early Power Labs. Both of us were fascinated with differentiation. We were particularly struck by the inability of Bottom groups to deal with differentiation. Time after time we would see the following scenario unfold: A powerful "We" almost instantaneously develops as soon as the Bottoms find one another. The language quickly becomes one of "We" rather than "I." There is an openhanded sharing of resources and information; there is a sense of the specialness of the group along with negative evaluations of all others ("humorously" hostile gibes aimed at the Elite and Managers). There is a palpable protective boundary around the group; there is a strong tendency to strategize and make decisions together. Unspoken norms develop regarding acceptable limits of behavior, and there is little or no individual action beyond those limits. Then the endless, and often painful, meetings begin. They start with high enthusiasm—ideas fly regarding possible action steps—but then energy runs down as the meetings drag on and on and on. Nothing can be decided. The differentiations emerge:

"Let's go on strike."
"It's too soon for that."
"Let's try to work the system."
"We're just being sucked in."
"The Elite seem reasonable."
"They're patronizing us."
"I'm happy to go on working."
"I'm not."

The "We" struggles for agreement ("If only I could make my position clearer, you would agree"), but agreement never comes. And soon the same patterns of arguments repeat themselves, and frustration and depression set in. [As we have seen in the previous case, sometimes this process is avoided by submerging one side of the conflict into invisibility and subsequent Village Idiocy.]

A Remarkable Transformation of Energy

In the early days of the Power Lab, we staff were inventing our roles as we went along, just as we were inventing the Lab. Sometimes we would be full-fledged players in one part of the system or another; at other times, we were nonintervening observers; at other times, we were rarely intervening kibitzers; and sometimes we were "Resource

Persons." In one program, Fritz was the designated Resource Person, which meant that he was available to all parts of the system.

One afternoon Fritz found himself in the middle of one of those downward-spiraling Bottom group discussions—

"Let's go this way."
"No, let's go that way."
"Let me explain why this way is the way to go."
"Let me try once again to show you how wrongheaded you are."

And on and on. Fritz stopped the conversation and said, with some enthusiasm, "It seems to me we have two teams here." And he made it sound as if these two teams were not competitors with one another but two units of the same team. "Why don't we see who is on which team?" And so the group began to divide. It was as if a jeweler had struck a diamond perfectly. Some members went quickly to one side or the other; they knew just where they stood. Others were more hard-pressed to choose, but in time, they all did. And then both groups went to work with this incredible release of creative energy. This transformation of energy was remarkable. What had seemed dead was now alive and cooking. What had seemed to be irreconcilable strategies now emerged as wholly compatible and complementary elements of one super-strategy. One group worked on constructing the new society—its constitution, judicial system, and so forth—while the other worked on strategies for getting the Elite's attention.

To us this instantaneous transformation seemed like a miracle—from dead to alive, from mutual blocking to mutual enhancement. And when we reviewed the process with participants, it was only with difficulty that they remembered Fritz's role in this. It all seemed so natural, as if it came out of them. *This was power*— influencing system energy.

What is striking about this is how in the Bottom Space, differentiations that are compatible and even potentially synergistic are experienced as irreconcilable. This is the illusion of the Bottom Space. Under the pressure of maintaining the integrity of the "We," differences that could coexist become enemies to one another. Great power comes to us when we recognize and move past the illusion—and great destruction often follows when we do not. Consider the splintering that happens within labor, among revolutionary groups, within religions.

■ ■ ■

Many years ago I was conducting a seminar for Christian military chaplains. Throughout the seminar, there was considerable tension between certain liberal and conservative chaplains. At one point, one chaplain said to another in frustration, "At least we can agree that we are brothers in Christ." And he stretched out his hand toward the other. But his hand just hung there in the air.

53 Creating Powerful Bottom Groups

In the Bottom group,
special attention needs to be paid to
individuation and differentiation.
In the environment of shared vulnerability,
individuation and differentiation will not come naturally;
they have to be worked at
rigorously.

1. Bottom groups are prone to function under the banner: In Unity There Is Strength. *A more powerful motto is: In Diversity There Is Strength.* Your challenge in the Bottom group is to surface both the diversity of your members and the diversity of your strategies and to integrate these diversities in the service of your system's mission.

2. *Encourage individuation.* In the Bottom group it is easy to hide in the "We"—to stand back and not put oneself at risk. Find out what different members bring to the party: What are their unique backgrounds, experiences, interests, and skills? Encourage members to step forward and use (risk) their uniqueness in the service of the group's mission.

3. *Encourage differentiation.* Develop simultaneous multiple strategies for pursuing your mission. If strategies appear contradictory, look more deeply. It is often an illusion of the Bottom Space that differences appear to be incompatible when they are not.

4. *Integrate regularly.* As you become more individuated and differentiated, the need for regular integration will increase. Meet regularly; share your experiences; coach one another on your various strategies.

Scene 3
The Politics of System Processes

All organic systems—from the split-leaf philodendron to the common earthworm to General Motors—engage in similar system processes. They individuate, integrate, differentiate, and homogenize. What distinguishes human systems from all other organic systems is that we think about these processes, we believe in them, we attach value to them, we politicize them, we favor one over the other.

54 Huddlers and Humanists . . . Enough With Consensus!

Some Words of Caution for Those Who Worship Togetherness

Sometimes
we *like* huddling—
thinking together,
planning together,
deciding together.
And sometimes
we *believe* in huddling.
Together
is the way we *should*
think,
plan,
decide
everything.
And so
we sit in our room
together
thinking,
planning,
deciding
everything.
An issue comes up.

Together
we think,
we plan,
we decide.
Another issue comes up
(there are three more at the door).
Together
we think,
we plan,
we decide.
Four new issues at the door,
six outside the window,
three opportunities just flew past
(waving bye-bye).
The issues flow in
under the door,
through the keyholes,
over the airwaves.
Our thinking grows fuzzy,
but still they come;
our planning is . . .
(What happened to planning?),
and still they come.
More issues:
Didn't we already handle that one?
Our decisions are random
(someone has to decide).

At least we're still together
thinking
(barely),
planning
(we'll get back to that),
deciding.

One of us rises,
goes to the window,
spies three golden opportunities flying by—
juicy opportunities—
so close, so close.
("Should one of us look into this?" he ventures.)
Should one?
Together
they think,
they plan,
they decide,
as the golden opportunities
fly lazily by
(bye-bye)
and six more issues
slide under the door.

Well . . .
at least we're
together.

55 Amebocytes and Slugs: The Politics of Individuation and Integration

Slime mold cells do it all the time . . . in each life cycle. At first they are single amebocytes swimming around, eating bacteria, aloof from each other, voting straight Republican. Then a bell sounds, and acrasin is released by special cells toward which the others converge in stellate ranks, touch, fuse together and construct the slug, solid as a trout. A splendid stalk is raised, with a fruiting body on top, and out of this comes the next generation of amebocytes, ready to swim across the same moist ground, solitary and ambitious. —Lewis Thomas, *The Lives of a Cell*[2]

He: Why are we talking about amebocytes and slugs?

She: Have you ever seen a more beautiful example?

He: Of what?

She: Individuation and integration. Isn't it beautiful?

He: I suppose it is.

She: Now let me ask you a question. What do you suppose would happen if the amebocytes decided to never come back?

He: I don't understand.

She: Say the amebocytes decided they never wanted to integrate again. They enjoy individuating. More than that, they believe in it. They want their freedom. They're against integration; they see it as constraining. So the amebocytes start carrying these placards saying: "Put an End to Big Government!" "Freedom Now!" "Deregulate the System!"

He: I don't see your point.

She: Or say the slug suddenly decides not to send out the next generation of amebocytes. The slug believes in integration. ("We're opposed to unrestrained individualism.") The slug is committed to the virtues of cooperation, loyalty, patriotism, connectedness.

He: Amebocytes and slugs don't think this way.

She: Maybe, maybe not. But who does think this way?

He: I think I'm getting the point.

She: I'm sure you are. We humans individuate and integrate. And we add a little extra to it. We attach values to these processes. We believe in them; they are the foundations of our organizations; we build political parties; we form governments; we even go to war around these processes.

He: Are you saying that with us it's the Slugs against the Amebocytes?

She: That's a nice way of putting it.

■   ■   ■

In his biography of John Kenneth Galbraith, Richard Parker states "These orthodox men [conservative economists] believed in markets [unbridled individuation] with a faith bordering on religion."[3] Parker states that in 1934 these economists opposed the early recovery efforts of the Roosevelt administration, "not on 'political' but on 'scientific' grounds."

Marxism was based on bogus science, as is the trickle-down theory of free market economics, as was slavery, the suppression of women, the exclusion of Asians and East Europeans, and worse. Greed, vengeance, scapegoating, domination all find welcome cover in bogus science.

If it's science you're after, I suggest you dig deeply into individuation and integration, amebocytes and slugs.

The Slugs Versus the Amebocytes

Slug Systems	Amebocyte Systems
The system comes first.	The individual comes first.
Loyalty, patriotism.	Freedom.
Align around the system's mission.	Do your own thing.
Amebocytes are selfish.	Slugs are oppressive.
Amebocytes produce chaos.	Slugs stifle creativity.
Amebocytes will destroy our system.	A Slug system isn't worth living in.
Amebocytes threaten traditional values.	Slugs cling to the past.
We must bring the Amebocytes into line or get rid of them.	We must get the Slugs off our backs.
Competition alienates Amebocytes from one another; it destroys their system.	Competition makes us great.

He: So it's good against evil.

She: Whichever side you stand on, there is an "evil empire" on the other side.

56 The Politics of Gender

She: If I asked you to match the following:

1. Male   a. Individuation

2. Female   b. Integration

What would you say?

He: I would say it would not be wise for us to get into this.

She: Good advice. Still, how would you match them?

He: *(hesitantly)* Well, the stereotype is Individuating Male, Integrating Female. The Hunter-Gatherer and the Maintainer-of-the-Campsite. But I'd prefer not to go much further with this.

She: Let us say, just for the purposes of discussion, that there is a consistent difference. Granting large areas of overlap and significant individual variation, let us say that males tend more toward individuation and females more toward integration.[4]

He: For the sake of discussion.

She: If there are differences, where is the problem? It's individuation and integration, it's amebocyte and slug—two indispensable system survival processes.

He: But that's not the way we talk about it.

She: Because we politicize the processes. Depending on where you stand, individuation and integration are either valued processes or disvalued ones.

Individuating Males	Integrating Females
Independent.	Connecting.
Strong.	Nurturing.
We do what needs to be done: the assertive actions.	We do what needs to be done: the maintenance actions.
Integrating females constrain us.	Individuating males disregard or abandon us. You are cold, detached, unfeeling.
We are rational, independent, objective. You avoid conflict.	We preserve intimacy.
You don't speak your mind.	You dominate the conversation.
Male individuation is what made our country great.	Male individuation is what led to colonialism, imperialism, war, and the oppression of women, people of color, and Native Americans.

She: So long as we politicize individuation and integration, it's impossible to create systems that recognize the contributions and limitations of both processes.

■ ■ ■

She: You look thoughtful.

He: Are some people pure amebocytes (individuators) and others pure slugs (integrators)?

She: Why do you ask?

He: I think I've seen them in our staff meetings.

Folie à Deux: Jack and Marianne

We're about to come to a decision. Jack (pure Individuator) listens as a consensus begins to form; he feels a familiar discomfort developing in himself, feels resistant to going along with the consensus, steps in and offers an opposing position, now feels more comfortable having established his separateness and opposition, and feels righteous in his position and opinion. The group now needs to deal with Jack's opinion. Some members simply see this as "Jack being Jack"; that is, consistently separate and oppositional. However, Marianne (a pure Integrator) is uncomfortable with Jack's action, with his opposition and potential separation from the group, and with the potential fraying of the group. Marianne's response is to be supportive of Jack, mollify him, and express appreciation for his courage and convictions—all of which is intended to keep Jack in, to prevent the group from dis-integrating. Little of this may have to do with any real agreement with or valuing of Jack's position. The rest of us roll our eyes.

He: Let's see if I have it. Jack is the Free Market system panicked by the imminent constraints of Socialism, while Marianne is pure Socialism desperately trying to fend off the chaos of Capitalism.

She: *(impressed)* So, whether it's an economic system, a political system, or an individual system, health comes from wholeness—individuation and integration.

He: Amebocyte and slug.

57 Or Would You Rather Be an Earthworm? Societal Implications of Differentiation and Homogenization

The earthworm
is a simple, generalized system—
little differentiation,
much homogenization.
The human organism
is a complex, specialized system—
much differentiation,
little homogenization.

Cut off the head of the earthworm,
and it grows a new head.
Cut off the human head,
and we're dead.

He: First amebocytes and slugs, now earthworms. What are you up to?

She: Differentiation and homogenization. These are two fascinating processes. Differentiation is about endless possibilities—system parts specializing, becoming increasingly different from one another.

He: And homogenization?

She: Homogenization is about commonality, replaceability. It's about system parts remaining similar to one another.

He: So?

She: These are two different strategies for system survival. One says: "Let's develop as great a variety among our parts as we can— even if our parts lose their commonality." The other says: "Let's maintain the replaceability of our parts even at the cost of variety."

He: I think I follow this, but what has this got to do with social systems . . . society . . . the BIG issues?

She: Most systems place their bets for survival on one process or the other. The earthworm is betting on homogenization at the expense of differentiation: Keep it simple, keep the parts replaceable. The earthworm is doing pretty well with its bet; it's been around for a lot longer than humans have.

The human organism has put its money on differentiation at the expense of homogenization—the body has an incredibly rich array of tools for interacting with the environment. The downside is our bodies are extremely vulnerable to the loss of key parts.

He *(impatiently)*: And so?

She: Homogenization without differentiation can be quite boring— like the earthworm.

He: I see that.

She: And differentiation without homogenization can be quite deadly.

He: And?

She: And that is what is happening to this single system called Humanity.

58 Differentiation: Inquiry or Warfare?

evolve *(i volv') v. To develop by a process of evolution to a different adaptive state or condition.*

Part of our job as Power Lab Anthropologists is to map the development of the system over time; this involves creating a series of diagrams capturing the shape of the system at various points—who is connecting with whom, what relationships are developing and which are breaking down, what structures are disappearing and what new ones are forming. As you stand in the Anthropologists' work area and take in the sequence of diagrams, you are struck with the beauty of the process: a system exploring its possibilities, searching for its natural structure; people searching for their places. (**14**, "Bart and Barb," provides a picture of this flowering process.) That is differentiation: the exploration of possibilities. Not truths, simply possibilities.

From the outside,
differentiation is beautiful;
from the inside,
it can be warfare.

From the outside,
it is open-ended inquiry;
from the inside,
it may feel like fixed and final truths.

From the outside,
it is "Let us explore all of the possibilities for this system."
From the inside,
it is "Let us pursue my way, the right way, the only True Way."

From the outside,
all possibilities seem worth exploring;
from the inside,
your possibility threatens the validity of my possibility.

From the outside,
there is an inevitability and beauty in our differentiations;
from the inside,
there may be pain and loss—

separation and divorce,

the dissolution of partnerships,

costly reorganizations,

abuse and oppression,

holy wars,

ethnic conflicts,

holocausts.

Are you telling me that the Truth is
one religion
or the other?
Are you telling me that the Truth is
one sexual orientation
or the other?
Are you telling me that the Truth is
big family or small
or none at all?
Expand or stand pat?
Black or white?
Fast or slow?
Your country or mine?
Now or later?
Hit 'em hard or be reasonable?
Your race or mine?

Such Truth exists on the inside;
from the outside
it's all inquiry.

He: You're treading on some dangerous ground here.
She: How is that?

He: You are diminishing everything we hold precious—my neighborhood, my country . . . my religion!

She: And how do I do that?

He: To you they are all options . . . possibilities . . . explorations. It could be this . . . but then again it could be that. You take away the specialness . . . My country right or wrong. You take away the possibility of belief. You call my religion a spiritual quest as if it's merely an option . . . one of several possibilities.

She: Isn't it that?

He: What if I think differently? What if I believe that it is the One True Religion?

She: Yes?

He: Well then, where will homogenization take me? If I ask myself what can be learned from exploring other spiritual quests, won't that change how I experience my religion?

She: I would hope so.

He: You would hope so!

She: I would hope so.

He: But won't it ruin it for me? I could never have the faith that I have now.

She: Maybe yes, maybe no. Who knows what you might discover? Maybe you would have a much deeper and richer faith than you have now. Does that ruin it? Or transform it?

He: Transform it?

She: From an answer to a continuing exploration. It is a big question after all. Transformation involves taking your quest to another level. There will be loss of the old certainties, but the new place may be a much more powerful one for you.

He: I feel the old dance shaking, and I don't know if I can handle this one.

She: It's your choice. It's always your choice.

59 An Ode to Homogenization

Differentiation yields national identity and pride;
and without homogenization,
it yields International Warfare.
Differentiation yields
richly varied religious expressions;
and without homogenization,
it yields Holy Wars.
Differentiation yields
ethnicity;
and without homogenization,
it yields Holocausts
and Ethnic Cleansing.
Differentiation yields
a variety of sexual orientations;
and without homogenization,
it yields Sexual Oppression.

Seeing involves
seeing what is
and seeing what is missing.
Wherever there is Differentiation,
we would do well to attend to Homogenization.
As we elaborate our differences,
we also need to develop and maintain our commonality.

Scene 4
The Challenge of Robust Systems

The Robust System is a vibrant, challenging,

and enriching place for its members to be in;

it is a system with outstanding capacity to

survive and thrive in its environment,

to cope with dangers

and prospect among opportunities.

But there is no Robust System

so long as there are

the Dominants

and the Others.

60 The Dominants and the Others

The Dominants and the Others
In many systems—
organizational and societal—
there are two cultures:
the Dominants
and the Others.
The Others exist within the Dominant culture:
females in male-dominant cultures,
acquired companies within the acquiring company,
people of color in a white-dominant society,
human resources in a marketing-dominant company
homosexuals in a heterosexual-dominant society,
Shiites in a Sunni-dominant society,
Sunnis in a Shiite-dominant society,
Christians in a Muslim-dominant society,
Native Americans in America,
devout Muslims in a secular society,

Palestinians in Israel,

Blacks in South Africa,

French-Canadians in English-Canadian–dominant society,

Muslims in a Buddhist-dominant society,

Serbs in the Ottoman Empire,

Jews in anti-Semitic societies,

Catholic, Japanese, Chinese, and other early immigrants in
the United States.

The Other

within the Dominant.

He: So we're not talking about "minorities"?

She: Minority, majority—that's not the issue. The question is,
whether it's organizational or societal, who has easier access to
the system's valued resources simply by virtue of being in the
dominant culture?

The Dominant Culture

The Dominants' culture

is invisible to them;

it is the water in which they swim,

the air they breathe.

To the Dominants,

how they speak

is the way one speaks,

how they dress

is how one dresses,

their values

are *the* values,

their history

is *the* history.

To the Dominants,
the culture of the Others
is not merely different,
it is wrong—
wrong speech,
wrong dress,
wrong emotionality,
wrong spirituality,
wrong values.
The culture of the Others is seen as strange,
sometimes comical,
usually lesser,
inferior.

The Dominants Act to Preserve Their Culture

The Dominants act to preserve their culture,
to protect it from being contaminated by the Other.
They stereotype the Other, seeing them as limited in ability,
intelligence, or morality;
they typecast the Other,
limiting them to roles that fit their stereotype;
they ignore or trivialize the accomplishments of the Other;
they exclude them
or marginalize them;
and in the extreme,
they enslave or exterminate them.

The Others Are Diminished (If Not Destroyed) in the Dominant Culture

To the Others,
the culture of the Dominants
is oppressive—
there is no space for *their* voice,
their dress,
their values,
their history.

Treated as second class,
the Others feel constrained, confused, shaky;
not knowing the rules of the Dominant culture,
they may feel incompetent and act incompetently,
or they may drop out
or drift into drugs and crime
or terrorism aimed at harming or destroying the Dominant
culture.
All of which reinforces the Dominants' stereotype of the
Others,
and reinforces the Dominants' efforts to preserve their
culture,
and on and on it goes.

The Situation Grows More Complex

Neither the Dominants nor the Others are uniform in their
reactions.
There is tension within both cultures.

Tension Within the Dominants

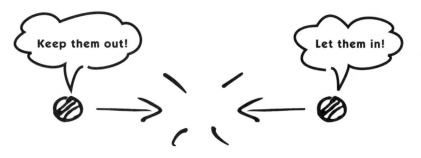

Within the Dominants there is tension
between the **Preserver/Protectors**
and the **Allower/Adapters**.
The Preserver/Protectors are a force for keeping the Others
out;
the Allower/Adapters are a force for allowing the Others in.
Preserver/Protectors and Allower/Adapters are in conflict
with one another over the appropriate way to deal with the
Others.

Tension Within the Other

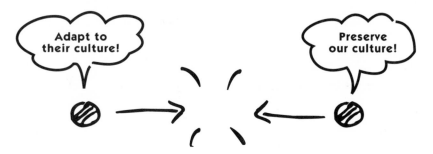

Within the Others there is tension
between the **Allower/Adapters** and the
Preserver/Protectors.
The Allower/Adapters are a force for entering the culture of
the Dominants.

The Preserver/Protectors are a force for resisting the Dominant culture and maintaining the purity of their own culture.

Allower/Adapters and Preserver/Protectors are in conflict with one another over how to relate to the Dominant culture.

The Purity "Solution"

Sometimes the Preserve/Protect voice becomes the predominant one among the Dominants; the Allow/Adapt voice is submerged. The Others are prevented from corrupting the culture of the Dominants. The Purity Solution takes many forms:

slavery, ghettos,

reservations, apartheid,

ethnic cleansing,

and genocide.

The Tolerance "Solution"

Sometimes the Allow/Adapt voice *is* heard:

some room is made for the culture of the Other within the Dominants;

their religion, language, music, practices *are* allowed;

yet the Dominant culture remains *the* Dominant culture,

and the Others remain the other:

present, not equal.

Tolerated.

He: So that's the choice: crush them or tolerate them?

She: There is another choice. The challenge of creating a robust system. And it *is* a challenge—a challenge that demands awareness and choice.

61 Robust System Processes

The Robust System—whether a family, a work team, an organization, a society, or a nation—is a high-energy system: members are using themselves fully, and the system as a whole is using itself fully, surviving and thriving in its environment, coping with dangers and prospecting among opportunities.

The system's energy comes from the interplay of apparently opposing forces.

It is a system in which members develop and express their uniqueness (individuation) and at the same time are team players (integration).

It is a system that welcomes and elaborates variety (differentiation) while working on commonality (homogenization).

It is a system that honors its traditions (preserve/protect) while exploring the new and unfamiliar (allow/adapt).

Individuation

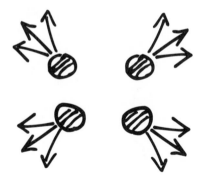

In the Robust System members use themselves fully; they develop and express their distinctive capacities—their unique interests, knowledge, skills, and abilities. They do not hide in the "We"; they continue to develop their individuality—to learn, to grow, to stretch, to be on the outer edge of their possibilities as human beings. These unique capacities then become their potential contributions to the system.

Integration

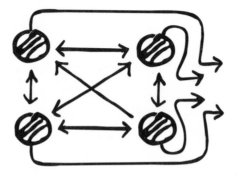

The Robust System has a powerful mission of the whole, a mission that is separate from the individual missions of its members and beyond what system members could accomplish alone. It is an inspiring mission—*What can this system do that has never been done before? What can we do better than it has ever been done before?* The mission gives members a larger sense of purpose; system members are committed to it; they value it and derive deep personal satisfaction from being a part of it and contributing to it. Members support one another in the service of the system's mission.

Differentiation

The Robust System zestfully elaborates differences; it develops variety in everything from types of cuisines to spiritual quests; forms of art, sport, entertainment, and education; products and services; forms of organizations; strategies for national defense; research interests; technology; and on and on. Just as system members become all that *they* can be, so does the Robust System becomes all that *it* can be. Differentiation provides a rich environment for its members—so many possibilities to experience—and it enables the system to interact complexly with its environment with a variety of structures and processes for coping and prospecting.

Homogenization

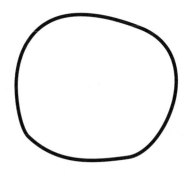

The Robust System zestfully pursues homogenization—processes by which members keep in touch with their commonality. There is a high degree of mutual understanding throughout the system; members work at understanding differences, whether these are functions in the workplace or belief systems in society.

Preserve/Protect (Stability)

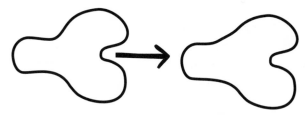

Elements of the Past Continuing into the Present

The Robust System values tradition: members are enriched by connecting with the system's history, its rituals, its accumulated wisdom. Tradition gives members the experience of being part of something larger than themselves, their place in an ongoing process. Tradition gives the Robust System stability and depth.

Allow/Adapt (Change)

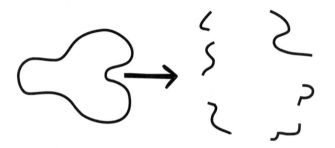

Elements of the Past Changing in Response to Present Conditions

The Robust System grows and changes; it values learning; it takes in information from its environment; it changes form and function in response to changing environmental conditions in order to continuously protect itself from danger and prospect among opportunities; it discards forms, processes, and beliefs that no longer connect with the current environment; and it experiments with new forms, processes, and beliefs.

Dominance and the Robust System

When there is a Dominant/Other scenario in play, Robust Systems are not a possibility.

The Dominants suppress individuation. Only behavior that fits the Dominant culture is acceptable.

The Dominants suppress differentiation. Only differences that fit the Dominant culture are acceptable.

The Dominants suppress change. Change is experienced as invalidating the Dominant culture.

The Dominant culture gradually disables itself by suppressing the contributions that individuation, differentiation, and change could make to the system's capacity to survive and thrive, cope and prospect in an ever-changing environment.

He: So let me see if I have this. Any system can be a Robust System—whether you're talking about society as a whole, an organization, or the Top, Middle, or Bottom systems within the organization. They're all candidates.

She: Right.

He: The trick is to be aware of what is happening to your system—

She: And what is not happening.

He: To not let yourself get stuck on one process or the other.

She: Right.

He: To zestfully pursue Individuation and Integration, Differentiation and Homogenization, Change and Stabilization.

She: Right.

He: I think I've got it.

62 The Dance of the Robust System: Ballet Notes

Summary of the Dance

The troupe enters the dance hall. They are the prototypical human system; they are the family, the work group, the team, the organization, the nation. They are in search of a mode of existence for themselves.

What kind of human system shall we be? There are at least six members in the troupe—three pairs—or, depending on the size of the production, there could be many more. In Act I their search takes them to unsuccessful experiences; first with Anarchy, then Totalitarianism, and finally Democracy. In Act II they succeed in creating the Dance of the Robust System—a dance that is integrated yet encourages individuation, a dance that is differentiated yet homogenized, a dance that carries on traditional forms while evolving into something new.

Act I. The Search

Anarchy: The Dance of Unrestrained Individuation

Each member is doing his or her own dance. There is liberty, freedom. The variety of dances is great. Each is beautiful in its own right, yet the overall effect is disconcerting. In time, chaos develops; the dances begin to interfere with one another. Conflicts and fights develop. Members tussle. Some withdraw, others sulk. Dancers fight with one another for space for their individual dances. Collisions increase. Frustration. Warfare. In the end, the dancers collide and collapse in a heap. Then a "solution" occurs to the dancers that leads them into the next dance.

Totalitarianism: The Dance of Unrestrained Integration

Chaos is eliminated. Members become one unit, perfectly synchronized. Everything is neat and orderly, not a person out of step. There are regimented marches, goose-stepping, tightly orchestrated configurations. This order is pleasing to the eye, especially following the chaos of the previous dance. Periodically a dancer breaks out of the pattern into an individual dance. These bursts of individuality are beautiful yet clearly out of place. They are quickly ridiculed, and the dancer is brought back into line. There is one exquisite individual performance that causes the others to stop and stare, first in admiration, then in anger. The exquisite dancer is finally shamed into conforming to the unit. The dance ends with all individuals brought back into line. There is a sadness to this. Then a new "solution" occurs to the dancers that leads them into the next dance.

Democracy: The Dance of Consensus

This is more of a debate about dance than a dance itself. The dancers discuss suggestions about which dance to engage in: Shall we dance this way or that way? There is considerable enthusiasm at the outset over particular possibilities; this is soon followed by much deliberation, criticism, nay-saying, suggested modifications, voting—all of which eventually drain the energy out of the dancers. Suggested dances become weaker, more tentative. Voting continues, apathy sets in. The dance ends in a vote; most dancers are by now so beaten down that they don't even vote, and the stage darkens.

Act II. The Robust System

Individuation and Integration

As the lights come up, all dancers are circling the stage, deep in thought, testing out snippets of dance, then rejecting them. One dancer bounds to the center of the stage, dancing powerfully in a way that captures the attention of others. There is a possibility here. The dancer invites the others to join. They do, one and two at a time. Some replicate the dancer's dance, others mirror the dancer, still others do their own dance while relating to the dancer. The dances are both unique and complementary, separate and connected.

The Dance of Differentiation

Different forms of dance develop, all connecting with the original dance yet taking their separate shape. Initially there is struggle: which form should the dance take, this *or* that? Struggle yields to agreement to pursue this *and* that, with enthusiasm and release of energy. Simultaneously, different dances emerge—the differentiated dances. These dances gradually develop in strength and beauty. In the end, we are treated to at least three very different and very beautiful dances going on simultaneously with an underlying common thread.

The Dances of Homogenization

The three differentiated dances continue. Dancers begin to get curious about one another's dances. *What are they doing over there?* In the following dances, members come together; they learn about the other dances, coach one another, and perform one another's dances.

Show Each differentiated dance is brought to the center and performed while the others observe.

Coach The dancers, in turn, coach one another on their dances and make suggestions as to how to strengthen each dance. There is exuberance in both the giving and taking of coaching.

Dances of the Whole Each differentiated dance group comes to the center and performs its dance; they are then joined by all the others; everyone learns to do every dance. There is a series of exuberant dances of the whole.

The Dance of the Robust System

In the finale, all of the elements of the Robust System are reprised and elaborated: the initial high-energy single dancer in solo, then others join with their unique ways of connecting with the dancer, then comes the emergence of the differentiated dances, followed by evidence of homogenization as dancers shift in and out of the differentiated dances. There are exuberant dances of the whole, and throughout, there are individual dances (previously suppressed dances are elaborated and honored). The ballet ends in an explosive burst of individuality and connectedness, difference and oneness, stability and change.

He: This is more than a dance for you, isn't it?

She: How do you mean?

He: This is your world vision, a vision of what is possible for us as human beings.

A world in which each of us develops and expresses our uniqueness

while working in common purpose with others;

a world that is rich in its variety

> while never losing sight of its common humanity,
>
> a world that is enriched by tradition
>
> while being ever curious and open to change.

She: If we can only see.

63 A Remarkable, If Somewhat Premature Epiphany

He: My God! I'm just beginning to see how big all of this is! You've just unraveled a gigantic mystery. Don't you see it? There is all this pain in the world—divorce, broken relationships, alienation. And it's all so stupid. It just doesn't have to be. None of it. We're just victims. We let it happen to us. Just because we don't see. It's all so clear and logical.

She: So?

He: So you've explained it to me, and now I want to explain it to others, to the world!

She: And how do you propose to do that?

He: It's all so clear. You just have to explain it to people. Show them how it all works. Show them the dances. Draw the pictures.

She: And?

He: And they'll see the light. They'll stop. They'll see how stupid they've been. How unnecessary all the pain has been.

She: *(with hint of sarcasm)* And that is just what people do best, isn't it? See how stupid they've been.

He: But it is all so clear! I've got the whole pattern. I'm ready to move. This is not deep. I have it all summarized on this card. I am ready to move out and make my fortune.

His Magic Consultant's Card

System	Pitfall	Need to Work On
Top	Over-Differentiated (Turf)	Integration and Homogenization
Middle	Over-Individuated (Alienation)	Integration
Bottom	Over-Integrated (GroupThink)	Individuation and Differentiation
Dominant/Other System	Over-Integrated Over-Homogenized Over-Preserved/Protected (Stability)	Individuation Differentiation Allow/Adapt (Change)

She: You may be right. For some people at least. There is some rationality in the world. You show them, and they'll see the light. A slap on the forehead. Aha! So that's the problem, and here's how to fix it—His Magic Consultant's Card.

He: Yes, and I am ready to move. I am going to alleviate a lot of pain in this world.

She: Yes, and I hope you do. But there is something you don't see.

He: Which is?

She: People are not just minds. They are not pure rationality. There is more at stake here than just seeing. People are emotional beings. They have investments in preserving the past and the present. They do not appreciate the possibility that they have been wrong. This is a very big deal. You must see that! What does it mean for me to have to accept the fact that my partnership did not have to fail, that my marriage did not have to fail, that these people I have such poor evaluations of might really be all right people, just like me. I have made investments in these feelings; I have justified them to myself many, many times in the past. And you, with your Magic Consultant's Card, you think that I will let go of all of that. Just because it makes sense!

He: Then what?

She: Do exactly what you said. But don't give up after the first "No," or the second, or the third. The greater the investment in the past—

He: The louder the sounds of the old dances shaking.

She: Exactly.

In this section, we have explored the costs of process blindness. We have seen how, in our blindness, we are vulnerable to the tugs of our environment; how we get stuck on certain processes to the neglect of others; how we passively and reflexively fall into nonproductive and destructive patterns of interaction—Turf Warfare, Alienation, and GroupThink. We have also seen how, in our blindness to system processes, we politicize these processes, valuing some and disvaluing others; and we have seen how, in so doing, we limit the power of our systems.

And we have explored the part dominance plays in diminishing the potential of our systems. Finally, we have explored the possibility of seeing system processes. When we see system processes, we can choose. We are driven neither by our system's environment nor by our politics. We can strive to create Robust Human Systems—systems in which we develop, respect, and encourage our individuality and our community, our diversity and our commonality, the depth of what we have been and our curiosity for what else we can be.

SEEING UNCERTAINTY

ACT IV

The truth makes for a bad sermon. It tends to be confusing and has no clear conclusion.

—*John Patrick Shanley*, Doubt: A Parable

The trouble with the world is that the stupid are cocksure and the intelligent full of doubt.

—*Bertrand Russell*

Life is full of uncertainties—conditions we face for which there are no clear-cut, objective, right-or-wrong answers or directions. *How does one raise children, punish murderers, handle unwanted pregnancies, respond to terrorism, express spirituality, deal with oppression, reduce crime, lead an organization or nation, reduce poverty? In short, how does one be in the world?*

Our human brains have limited tolerance for uncertainty, and so, with great regularity, conflicting positions and factions arise whose adherents are fortified with certainty and righteousness: they are firmly pro-choice *or* pro-life, for capital punishment *or* against it, for preemptive war *or* opposed to it, for gay marriage *or* against it, moderate in their approach to change *or* radical, liberal in their social policy *or* conservative, committed in their spiritual beliefs as Catholics *or* Protestants *or* Jews *or* Muslims *or* atheists, and on the list goes.

Certainty eliminates the angst of uncertainty; beyond that, it leads to the inevitable battle of certainty versus certainty. The costs of such conflicts range from mild to catastrophic; from hurt feelings and tense relationships to polarized neighborhoods, constitutional struggles, and divisive political campaigns, to wars—holy and otherwise—and, in the ultimate, to genocides and holocausts.

In Act IV, we will focus primarily on the fundamental uncertainty underlying many of the conditions we face in organizational life. We will see how our reflex to escape from uncertainty limits the contributions we can make to our systems and leads us into unnecessary and destructive battles with one another. We will explore how facing uncertainty and working with it can generate transformative possibilities for ourselves and our systems.

In **Scene 1**, our focus will be on the challenges we face as individuals in the presence of organizational uncertainty.

In **Scene 2,** our focus will be on the experience of groups in the presence of organizational uncertainty.

In **Scene 3**, we will venture beyond organizational life to examine uncertainty and our responses to it in broader aspects of social system life.

64 The Emergence of Organizational Positions

She: We get up every morning and head off for work;

we have our titles, job descriptions, responsibilities;

we are bolstered by years of education, training, and experience;

we enter our worlds

and encounter . . .

uncertainty.

He: Uncertainty?

She: Uncertainty. No schoolbook answers, no simple solutions to the complex conditions we face.

Only uncertainty.

■ ■ ■

Despite appearances of clarity, purpose, direction, and stability, *organizations are fundamentally worlds of uncertainty*, whichever position one enters, there is total uncertainty as to how one is to proceed—no universal answers, directions, or guidelines. Yet organizations don't appear to be befogged by uncertainty, because fundamental uncertainties are immediately papered over with veneers of order—rules, procedures, traditions, principles—provided by history (*This is how we've always done it*), theory (*Leading authorities say this is how to proceed*) or personal beliefs (*This is what I think, or what my religion or philosophy says is the correct way to proceed*). Still, beneath this surface order and clarity there remain, generally unexplored, the fundamental uncertainties of organizational life.

Scene 1
Individuals in Uncertainty

65 Individuals Facing and Escaping from Organizational Uncertainty

Top in Uncertainty

Top world of complexity and accountability

When I enter the Top world—as a top executive, or parent, or plant manager, or business partner—I accept overall responsibility for the system—the organization, family, plant, or business. The entire system is in my hands, with fundamental questions facing me: What kind of system to fashion? What culture to foster? How fast to grow? What risks to take?

There are no obviously correct answers to these questions.

In the face of uncertainty there are only possibilities: I *could* be conservative or I *could* be expansive; I *could* be hard with system members or I *could* be soft; I *could* be egalitarian or I *could* be hierarchical. Nothing but possibility. No answers.

We humans have little tolerance for uncertainty, so (not all of us, not every time, but with great regularity) we escape into certainty. One possibility becomes *the* possibility. It becomes my *position*. Now I am a firmly committed expansive . . . or conservative . . . or egalitarian . . . or hierarchical.

In some sense it makes little difference which position I adopt; the main point is to escape from uncertainty.

He: What do you mean *It makes little difference?* Of course it makes a difference.

She: Maybe less than you think.

Bottom in Uncertainty

Bottom world of vulnerability

When I am living in the Bottom world, I am living in *their* system; I am facing a condition of vulnerability; these others make decisions that influence my life in major and minor ways.

There are no obviously correct answers as to how to manage my vulnerability, only possibilities: I could accept their system and live within it; on the other hand, I could try to change their system in moderate or more extreme ways.

Nothing but possibility. No answer. Anxiety. Intolerable, so I escape— (not all of us, not every time, but with great regularity). One possibility becomes *the* possibility, my firm position. Now I am a committed radical . . . or moderate . . . or adapter.

It makes little difference which I become; the main point is I have escaped from uncertainty.

Middle in Uncertainty

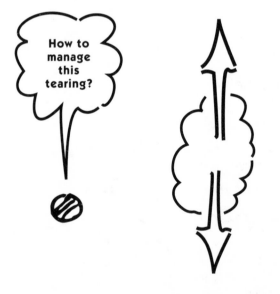

Middle world of tearing

As a Middle I am living in a tearing world, existing among the often conflicting perspectives, priorities, needs, and demands of others.

There are no obviously correct answers as to how to manage this tearing, only possibilities: I could alleviate tearing by primarily focusing on serving those above me (after all, they *do* pay my salary); on the other hand I could alleviate the tearing by focusing primarily on serving those below me (they're the ones I depend on to get the work done); still again, I could do my darnedest to serve all parties to their satisfaction (and probably burn out in the process); and on the other hand I might protect myself from being abused by any of them. Align up, align down, burn out, bureaucratize. All possibilities. Not a comfortable position to be in. I escape into certainty (not all of us, not every time, but with great regularity). One possibility becomes *the* possibility, my firmly held position. Now I am a committed upwardly aligned Middle . . . or a downwardly aligned one . . . or a bureaucratized one. It makes little difference; whichever way I go, I have succeeded in escaping from uncertainty.

Dominant and Other in Uncertainty

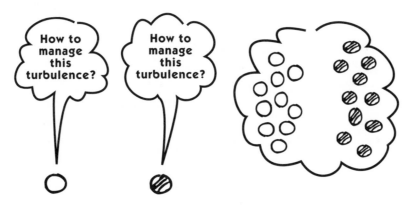

The meeting of cultures

As Dominant or Other, I am facing turbulent conditions caused by the meeting of cultures.

How can I manage this turbulence? Again, there are no answers, only possibilities. I could avoid turbulence by keeping my culture separate from the other; on the other hand, I could simply allow the cultures to meet and live with—tolerate—whatever happens.

No clear-cut path to follow, only the anxiety of uncertainty. I escape from uncertainty (not all of us, not every time, but with great regularity). One possibility becomes *the* possibility, my firm position. Now I am a committed preserve/protector, dedicated to keeping my culture from being contaminated by the Other or an equally committed allow/ adapter solidly in favor of allowing the cultures to meet. It makes little difference which position I hold; each serves me equally well in escaping from uncertainty.

He: (*agitated*) This time you have definitely gone too far.

She: What's the problem?

He: That it makes no difference which position you adopt.

She: You feel otherwise?

He: Of course I do. *Values matter.* We choose on the basis of loyalty or justice or self-interest. You're saying *It could be this or it could be that.* That's not the way we experience it. We care a great deal about which way we go.

She: That is precisely the point. We do care and values do make a difference.

He: (*relieved*) I'm glad you agree.

She: And so do other things. Interaction comfort matters. We may opt for allow/adapt not out of any particular values, but because we are uncomfortable in saying No, in keeping others out. Likewise, we could opt for preserve/protect—again, not out of any value, but because we are uncomfortable interacting with others.

He: I can see that.

She: And economic interests matter. We may keep the Other out because it is in our economic interest to do so, or let them in for the same reason.

He: So it does make a difference which way you go.

She: Fundamentally, it doesn't. Values, economic interests, interaction comfort—they all matter in that they solidify our escape from uncertainty with fine righteous underpinnings. But it's the escape that counts, however we manage it.

He: I'm not convinced. Still, if we didn't escape from uncertainty, what would we do? How would we begin?

She: With a mutant moment.

66 A Mutant Moment in the Middle

Throughout this book, we have seen various cases of mutant moments: situations in which the familiar dance took an unfamiliar turn; it didn't go the way it usually goes (see **26**, "Daniel in the Middle," and **23**, "Let's Declare Bankruptcy"). Mutant moments inevitably produce turbulence—the old dance shaking—yet in the end they have the potential to produce results that are empowering for the actor and the system.

Barry may have had such a mutant moment in the Power Lab. Let's look at it and see what light it can shed on the challenges and opportunities of uncertainty.

■   ■   ■

Elsewhere I have told the story of my adventures as a Middle in the Power Lab.[1] How I entered nervously, concerned that, given my writing on the Middle condition and the fact that I was the developer of the Power Lab, others would both be suspicious of me and expect great things from me. There is a piece I'd like to add that relates to the matter of uncertainty.

It begins with the sleeplessness I experienced the first night of the program. That afternoon the Elite had given me my orientation and assignment. It was clear what my job was—Manager of Facilities (including food, the store, and housing) plus Court Officer and Manager of the Pub. What was not clear was what kind of Manager I would be.

Consider the Middle condition I was entering: The Elite controlled all the society's resources: the bank, the housing, the food supply, the court system, employment opportunities, my salary, and more; the Immigrants were about to enter with little more than the clothes on their backs; and I was to exist somehow between the two. How would I be? Would I be aligned with the Elite or with the Immigrants? Would I work closely with my associate Middles or go it alone? What struck me, and kept me awake a good part of the night, was the realization that I could be any of these. There was no obviously correct answer to how to be in the Middle. I could be a cracker-jack Middle in the service of the Elite, carrying out my assignments diligently and elegantly. After all, the Elite were paying my salary, and they were the owners of this property. I could also have a very different existence as an advocate of the Immigrants, working on their behalf to achieve greater equality, power, and shared ownership. There was still another possibility: I could quit my job and take my chances as a hobo in the society.

The reader may be feeling that certain choices are obviously correct [She: Pay attention to that impulse to jump to certainty]; *but this was not my experience. I experienced them all as possibilities; for me there was no obviously correct way to be. All that was available was choice. This was not a comforting insight. In the face of pure uncertainty, my experience was anxiety.* [She: And it is that experience of anxiety—or the impulse to avoid it—that regularly propels us into the comfort of one position or another.]

Experiencing the uncertainty, however, living in it for even a few hours (a few hours in the Power Lab may be the equivalent of weeks or months in normal time) had an effect that I could only vaguely grasp. The Middle whom I became in that Power Lab was outside of any of the options I had been considering. I aligned neither with the Elite nor with the Immigrants; I did drop out [She: Pay attention to that.], *but just for an hour or so, and then reentered with a fundamentally different way of being Middle. I don't think I could have put words around it at the time, but in retrospect, it was about establishing—with my Middle colleague— an independent Middle position that was not the servant of either Top or Bottom, yet could provide valuable services to both and to the system as a whole, while allowing the two of us the opportunity to use our unique perspective, skills, and resources.*

I cannot overstate how both exhilarating and frightening this new possibility was. [She: Notice, a new level of uncertainty.] *Could we actually be this way in this system? Could we survive? Could we pull this off? In the framework of the current conversation, I and my partner were deep into the uncertainty of Middleness.*

We did survive, and the transformation, particularly for those of us who have studied the Middle position for many years, was mind-boggling. This was not a minor modification of how it usually goes; it was a totally different realm of experience. Here is how I described it in Leading Systems:

Generally, [the Middle House] is a barren, unexciting place. It is quiet; if Middles are there, they are usually off by themselves organizing their paperwork for their particular areas of responsibility. There is very little action, still less interaction, no smells of food, no visitors dropping in just to chat . . . and no fun. Absolutely no fun.

Oasis (the name we gave to our transformed Middle house) was quite another story. It became the center of community life. The aromas of food cooking on the stove filled the house [how we got food is its own story; see "Begging with Barry" in Leading Systems]; people ate; they took some of the warm clothing we had put out; they came in just to chat; they participated in several seminars the Immigrants offered; we had dancing lessons. Food, clothing, shelter, respite, education, and entertainment. Oasis was the hottest spot in town, a triumph for us Middles. Innovation, contribution, entrepreneurship, and partnership. Not the way it usually goes in the Middle.

Living from Uncertainty to Greater Uncertainty

Barry's mutant tale is hardly a story of one well-planned move after another; rather, it is a tale of uncertainty followed by uncertainty followed by uncertainty. When finding himself in the Middle, he is uncertain as to how to *be* Middle. He experiences the usual possibilities, but no one of them draws him more strongly than any other. The realization that everything is possible yet nothing is compelling only adds to his anxiety and uncertainty. Not having resolved anything, he makes his way as best he can. In time, he feels that *whatever he is doing is not working for him*; he is not fully satisfying Tops or Bottoms, nor himself.

It may be that for many of us in the Middle that same experience of falling short for everyone *would* be unhappily acceptable. *Isn't that what it is to be Middle?* Barry, however, drops out; temporary relief—the absence of tearing—is once again followed by uncertainty and anxiety (*What to do? How to survive?*). In the uncertainty and anxiety, another possibility emerges that is both exhilarating and frightening. *What if we* can *make this Oasis business happen? What if we* can't *make this happen? This is not what anyone—Top or Bottom—expects of us as Middles.*

The image that is forming for Barry is a way of being Middle far outside the familiar options of align-up, align-down, bureaucratize, or burnout. *It is about being independent Middles, operating from their own independent perspectives, using their unique skills, for the purpose of empowering themselves and contributing to the system.*

That way of being Middle does not eliminate uncertainty; it simply moves uncertainty to a new level of what Middles can be and what they can contribute.

■　■　■

He:　Is this just a Barry story or is there a larger lesson here?

She:　It may be that the lesson is to live with uncertainty and then, if we are patient and aware, we can move to a new level of uncertainty.

He:　A new level of uncertainty? That's the good news?

She:　The very good news. But we need to revisit the Dance of Blind Reflex to see how it has brought us into these Tunnels of Limited Options.

67 Dancing in and out of the Tunnel of Limited Options

The Dance of Blind Reflex brings us into the Tunnel of Limited Options, and it is our awareness of the dance that can lead us out.

She: Let's review:

As Top, I reflexively draw responsibility up to myself and away from others. That response takes me into the Top Tunnel of Limited Options, in which my belief is: I am responsible for the system's fate, and my options are limited by that belief.

My Belief in the Top Tunnel of Limited Options

As Bottom, I reflexively hold higher-ups responsible for my condition and the condition of the system. That response takes me into the Bottom Tunnel of Limited Options, in which my belief is that *Others are responsible for my fate and the fate of the system,* and my options are limited by that belief.

My Belief in the Bottom Tunnel of Limited Options

As Middle, I reflexively slide in between others' issues and conflicts and make them my own. That response takes me into the Middle Tunnel of Limited Options, in which my belief is that *My business is to service others,* and my options are limited by that belief.

My Belief in the Middle Tunnel of Limited Options

As Dominant or Other, I reflexively act to reduce turbulence generated by the meeting of our culture with another. That response takes each of us into the Dominant/Other Tunnel of Limited Options, in which we share the belief that *My business is to protect my culture against chaos,* and our options are limited by that belief.

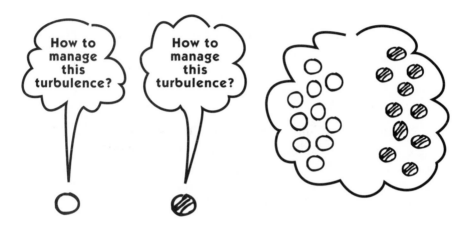

**My Belief (as Dominant or Other) in the Dominant/Other
Tunnel of Limited Options**

Once in these tunnels, we can see only options that are consonant with these beliefs. *We cannot see the more powerful options that lie outside the tunnel.*

He: I'm not sure I understand.

She: Take Barry's case. Inside the tunnel, the belief is *My business is to service others.* Given that belief, options are limited to the usual suspects: align-up, align-down, try to please everyone, bureaucratize. Only as that belief was questioned did that more powerful way of being Middle emerge.

He: I understand, but how does that happen for the rest of us? How do we get out of the tunnel? How do we discover those more powerful options?

She: You're the consultant with the Magic Card; maybe you're the one who can help people out, who can help them become aware of the dance.

He: I can do that.

She: And maybe it happens without you; it happens when people realize that what they are doing is just not working for them.

He: That was Barry's experience. *It just wasn't working.*

She: And maybe people just stop and tarry a while in the uncertainty and see what emerges.

Questions Emerge

In the uncertainty, important questions may emerge.

In the Top tunnel: Why am *I* responsible for this system's fate?

In the Bottom tunnel: Why is my fate in *their* hands?

In the Middle tunnel: Why is it my function to service *others*?

In the Dominant/Other tunnel: Why am I running from turbulence?

With these questions, we find ourselves out of the Tunnels of Limited Options; we are observing ourselves, we are noticing how we have responded to the conditions we have been facing, and we are now in a position to choose differently.

Uncertainties Emerge

And it's with those questions that new uncertainties emerge:

If I am not a Top who sucks up responsibility, who am I when I am Top?

If I am not a Bottom who holds others responsible for my fate and the fate of the system, who am I when I am Bottom?

If I am not a Middle whose function is to service others, who am I when I am Middle?

If I am not a Dominant or Other who protects my culture from chaos, who am I when I am Dominant and Other?

New Empowering Possibilities Emerge for Us

If we are willing to face this new level of uncertainty, then new possibilities become available to us—possibilities that are both exhilarating and anxiety-producing, possibilities that move uncertainty to a new level of what we can be and what our systems can be. These possibilities await us outside the tunnels; we may see them or we may remain blind to them; we may see them but choose to ignore them. But they are there.

As Top, instead of sucking responsibility up to myself and away from others, and being responsible for the system's fate,

my challenge is to be a Top who creates a system that is responsible for its own fate.

As Bottom, instead of holding *them* responsible for my condition and the condition of the system,

my challenge is to be a Bottom who is responsible for my own fate and who shares in responsibility for the fate of the system.

As Middle, instead of losing myself—my unique perspective and resources—in the service of others,

my challenge is to be a Middle who maintains my independence of thought and action and uses it in the service of the system.

As Dominant or Other, instead of protecting my culture from the turbulence caused by the meeting of another culture,

my challenge is to be a Dominant or Other who uses that turbulence as a basis for creating a new culture more robust than either of the existing ones.

These challenges are not simple adjustments to organizational life as we know it. They are fundamental shifts in what it is to *be* Top, Middle, Bottom, Dominant, and Other. Fundamentally different agendas for how we handle the continuing complexity at the top, vulnerability on the bottom, tearing in the middle, and turbulence in the meeting of cultures.

And New Possibilities Emerge for Our Systems

Living from these stands challenges us to become more of what *we* can be as individuals; and it is also true that they challenge our systems to become more of what *they* can be.

Each of these stands exists as a design principle for our organizations; each works with the others, and each strengthens the system, building its capacity to survive and thrive in its environment.

Consider the power of a system in which:

At whatever level we are Top, we are using our positions to create responsibility throughout those systems for which we are Top;

at whatever level we are Bottom, we are taking responsibility for our condition and sharing responsibility for the condition of the system;

at whatever level we are Middle, we are using our unique perspectives and resources in the service of the system;

and as Dominants and Others we are working together to create new cultures more robust than either of theirs.

That is the possibility of life outside the Tunnel of Limited Options.

He: This is great. I am ready to roll. I'm a consultant who helps people *see* the dance, *escape* the dance, and create more powerful possibilities for themselves and their systems. There is, however, just one more thing I need from you.

She: What?

He: A list of *hows*.

How do we be Tops who create responsibility?

How do we be Bottoms who accept our responsibility for ourselves and the system?

How do we be Middles who maintain our independence of thought and action?

How do we be Dominants and Others who work together to create a robust culture?

Let's have the list, and I'll be off.

She: Sorry. No list. With these challenges, we end where we began: uncertainty. There are no clear-cut road maps for how we carry out any of these. They will draw on us to grow, to develop new resources, to create new partnerships, and to resist the unyielding lure of the Dance of Blind Reflex. If we are committed to the stands—and that is the key—we will find our *hows*.

He: They *will* want the hows.

She: And they *will* find them . . .

He: *If* they are really committed to the stands.

She: Exactly. First, choose to *be*; then the hows will follow.

68 His Magic Consultant Card #2

From Uncertainty to Power

He: (*excited*) I now see the whole picture, and I am ready to get out there and make a huge difference in the world.

She: Let's see what you have this time.

He: (*revealing his Magic Consultant Card #2*) It starts with fundamental uncertainty: how to manage the conditions we are in.

        Then the Dance of Blind Reflex takes us into the Tunnel of Limited Options and keeps us there.

        In the Tunnel, we do battle with one another about how best to manage these conditions. Certainty versus certainty. Position versus position.

        These battles are costly. They result in personal stress, breakdown in relationships, loss of potential partnerships, and the weakening of the system.

Hope comes with insight, with the ability to see and work with uncertainty.

With a nudge from me, people will recognize what is keeping them hooked in the Tunnel.

And then, out of the Tunnel they come, with powerful ways of being in those conditions.

How can this fail? I'm ready to roll.

She: What are you planning to do?

He: Everything you've taught me: systemic awareness and choice. I'll help people see clearly and then choose wisely.

She: Slow down. Think about what this means. Some people may not be eager or ready for life outside the Tunnel.

As Bottoms, we are faced with being responsible for our own fate. That's a huge step away from holding others responsible for our fate.

And I may not want to take that step.

I enjoy blame.

I find satisfaction in being the victim.

Being responsible is just too much work.

Thanks, but I think I'll stay right here.

Outside the Tunnel,

as Middles, we are challenged with maintaining our independence of thought and action. That's a huge step away from being solely responsive to others' needs, agendas and priorities.

And I may not want to take that step.

No one wants me to be independent; they all want me to do what they want me to do.

It's hard to push back on others, especially my Top.

I'll get fired for being independent.

I like the importance of being needed by everyone.
Thanks for the offer, but I'll stay right here.

Outside the Tunnel,

as Tops, we are challenged with creating a system that is responsible for its own fate. That's a huge step away from being the one who is responsible for the system's fate.

And I may not want to take that step.

I'm afraid things would get out of control.

I know how to suck up responsibility; I know less about how to create a responsible system.

Others will see me as weak.

I will lose my importance.

Thanks for the offer, but I'll stay right here.

Outside the Tunnel,

in the meeting of cultures, we are challenged to accept and work with turbulence toward creating a system more robust than that of the Dominants or the Others. That's a huge step away from protecting our cultures against turbulence.

And I may not want to take that step.

It's easier just to let what happens happen.

It's easier just to stay separate from the other culture.

Thanks for the offer but I'll keep my position.

My point is: These are not minor shifts in behavior.

He: So what do I do?

She: Do what you plan to do, and expect resistance.

He: Aha! Is it resistance? Or is it simply the sound of the old dance shaking?

His Magic Consultant's Card II

	Bottom	Middle	Top	Cultural Meeting
Fundamental Uncertainty	How to manage our vulnerability to "Them."	How to manage this tearing.	How to manage this responsibility.	How to manage the turbulence of the coming together of cultures.
The Dance of Blind Reflex	I hold others responsible for my fate and the fate of the system.	I slide in between others' issues and conflicts and make them my own.	I suck up responsibility to my self and away from others.	I protect my culture from turbulence.
Belief That Takes Us and Keeps Us in the Tunnel of Limited Options	My fate is in their hands.	My business is to service others.	The fate of this system is in my hands.	Turbulence will weaken my culture.
Options in the Tunnel	Adapt or Be Moderate or Be Radical	Align-up or Align-down or Bureaucratize or Burn out	Expand or Conserve * Equality or Hierarchy * Hard or Soft	Allow/Adapt or Preserve/Protect
Illumination in the Tunnel	Why have I tied my fate to "Them"?	Why am I only focused on what others see and want?	Why am I deciding these important issues?	Why am I protecting my culture?
The Key to Getting Out of the Tunnel	To unhook from my dependence on "Them."	To unhook from the focus on what others want.	To unhook from my being the determiner of this system's fate.	To unhook from protecting my culture from turbulence.
Powerful Stands in the Fresh Air	I am responsible for my own condition and the condition of the system.	I stay focused on what I see the system needs and on what I uniquely bring to it.	I work on creating a system that is responsible for its own fate.	I work on creating a robust system.

Scene 2
Groups in Uncertainty

69 # Groups Facing and Escaping from Uncertainty

She: So now let's see what happens (*not always, not with everyone, but with great regularity*) when collections of us come together in these Top, Middle, Bottom, and cultural meeting spaces.

He: I think by now I see the tragedy about to unfold.

She: So draw it out for us.

He: Perfectly nice collections of people gather;

each collection—Tops, Middles, Bottoms, Dominants, and Others—enters its space of uncertainty;

possibilities emerge;

possibilities harden into positions.

She: And then the drama begins.

Top Groups: from Uncertainty into Polarization

We started off together in that top world, facing the fundamental uncertainty about how to manage our collective responsibility for the system. No obviously correct "solution" to the complexity we faced. Nothing but possibilities. But now our possibilities have transformed into fixed and firm oppositional positions. The following gives a flavor of some of the recurring positional struggles that we are now facing:

Expansives versus **Conservatives,**

Egalitarians versus **Hierarchicals,**

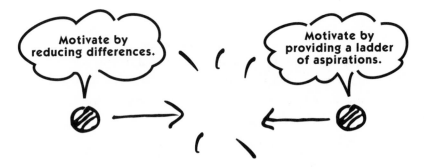

Hards versus **Softs.**

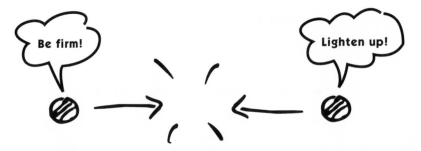

Expansives driving for growth feel constrained by **Conservatives;**
Conservatives trying to maintain stability feel endangered by

Expansives (see **40**, "The Success of a Business, the Failure of Its Partners").

Hards, driving to set high performance standards for system members, see **Softs** as weakening members and lowering the quality of performance; **Softs** striving for congenial relationships with system members see **Hards** as unnecessarily alienating these members.

Egalitarians driving to motivate by reducing differences see **Hierarchicals** as insisting on dysfunctional barriers; **Hierarchicals** striving to create clarity in duties and responsibilities see **Egalitarians** as blurring boundaries and weakening authority.

These struggles produce stress for individual Tops; they cause relationships to fray and often fracture; they produce tension throughout the system (*the Tops are fighting!*), and they drain energy away from the business Tops should be doing. These relationships often end in painful and costly divorces (business or family) as the partners agree that they can no longer exist together.

Bottom Groups: From Uncertainty into Opposition

In the Bottom world we all faced the same fundamental uncertainty about how to manage our vulnerability. Again, no obvious "solutions," just possibilities. In time, flexible possibilities morphed into fixed positions of certainty: **Adapters** versus **Moderates** versus **Radicals**.

Now there are tensions between **Adapters,** choosing to accept the system and work within it, and **Moderates** and **Radicals,** both of whom are oriented to changing the system, albeit by different means—**Moderates** softer in their approach, and **Radicals** harder. **Moderates** experience **Radicals** as too extreme in their efforts and therefore counterproductive, **Radicals** experience **Moderates** as too fainthearted and therefore counterproductive, and both experience **Adapters** as naively perpetuating an unjust system, while **Adapters** see both—but especially the **Radicals**—as troublemakers threatening to increase rather than reduce their vulnerability.

The tensions between members range from mild—in which parties argue with, try to convince, and protect themselves from one another—to explosive: strikes in company towns in which **Adapters**, **Moderates**, and **Radicals** fight with one another, friendships end, towns are divided; as well as in revolutionary movements in which **Radicals** kill **Moderates**, as was the case in the Russian revolution, the Iraq war, and Rwanda and Burundi. Cases in which the leap from uncertainty to certainty has had disastrous consequences.

Middle Groups: From Uncertainty into Alienation

In the Middle world, we were all faced with the same fundamental uncertainty about how to manage this tearing between the conflicting priorities, perspectives, and demands of others. Out of that place of no certain "solutions," fixed positions have emerged. Tensions between the **Upward-Aligned** Middles, who see themselves as primarily in the service of those above them, the **Downward-Aligned**, who see themselves as primarily in the service of those below them, the **Burnouts**, who see their mission as serving everyone, and the **Bureaucrats**, who resolve their tearing by protecting themselves against all.

These "resolutions" of this tearing have further alienated Middles from one another. Integration among the Middles is an unlikely prospect. The **Downward-Aligned** see the **Upward-Aligned** as management toadies; the **Upward-Aligned** see the **Downward-Aligned** as lacking the right management stuff. Both see the **Bureaucrats** as hostile barriers, and all see the **Burnouts** as well-intentioned but ineffective in the long run. All are evaluative of one another's positions.

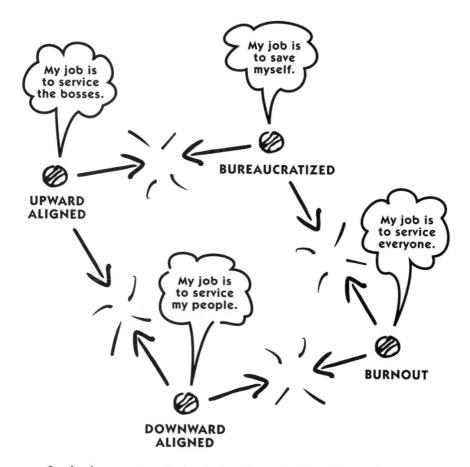

In the documentary Power Lab: Living in New Hope *there is a scene that neatly illustrates this condition. There has been a protest in the form of a sit-in in the dining room. Several Immigrants are on the floor refusing to leave. One Middle is on the floor, firmly committed to the Immigrants' position; standing directly above her is another Middle, doing his best to enforce the Elite's order; and off to the side are other Middles, eating their dinner and watching as if all of this has little to do with them.[2]*

Dominants and Others: From Uncertainty into Polarization

The Dominants and the Others all faced the same uncertainty about how to manage the turbulence caused by the meeting of their cultures.

No obvious "solutions." Again, no textbook answer, only uncertainty. Yet out of this uncertainty, fixed oppositional positions emerged.

Now, within both cultures there are tensions between the **Preserve/Protectors**, who want to protect their culture from being contaminated by the other, and the **Allow/Adapters**, who want to allow the cultures to meet.

Within the Dominants, The **Preserve/Protectors** view the **Allow/Adapters** with disdain, as "liberals" contributing to the debasing of their culture, and the **Allow/Adapters** treat the **Preserve/Protectors** as "conservative" relics, stuck in the past and unable or unwilling to cope with change.

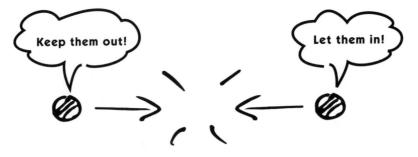

Within the Others, The **Preserve/Protectors** see the **Allow/Adapters** as selling out to the Dominant culture—gays acting straight, women acting mannish, Jews blending in with Christians. The **Allow/Adapters** see the **Preserve/Protectors** as reinforcing stereotypes that make the integration of the **Allow/Adapters** difficult.

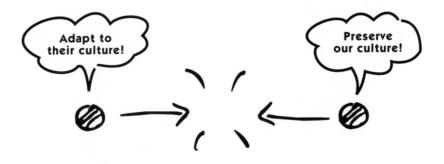

He: This makes me very uncomfortable. All these positions battling with one another. It's everywhere: in the organization, in the culture, on radio, television, op-ed pages of the newspaper, in the elections. Everywhere. It's nothing but certainty against certainty. Matters you can't even discuss.

She: To open these to discussion runs the risk of taking you back to uncertainty.

He: It's a feeling that we're all in the dark, making up stories, acting like we really know the truth, but we're just grasping at half-truths, simplicities. We're taking this immense complexity of the world we're stumbling through and reducing it to a set of sound bites. What makes it scary is that we're all so sure.

She: For many of us uncertainty is scary. The real work lies in accepting uncertainty and working with it.

70 How to Transform Oppositional Struggles into Multifaceted Flexible Teams

Teach thy tongue to say "I don't know." —Maimonedes

The key to resolving firm oppositional positions lies in all parties recognizing that beneath these apparent certainties lie fundamental uncertainties.

She: The tragedy for ourselves and our systems is that none of these oppositional struggles needs to happen. We are like fragile eggshells; just confront us with uncertainty and we crack into these separate oppositional pieces.

He: *All the king's horses and all the king's men couldn't put Humpty Dumpty together again.*

She: So much for the power of kings and their horses, but we *can* put these pieces together.

He: And just how do we do that?

She: The first step is to recognize that we are stuck in our Tunnels of Limited Options fighting with one another, when we could and should be outside the Tunnel working *together* to deal with the uncertainties we are facing.

He: That's a huge first step, especially when we are firmly locked into the righteousness of our positions.

She: That's right; it will take nothing less than our becoming Masters of Uncertainty.

How to Master Uncertainty

1. **Accept the fundamental uncertainty.** As a starting point, all of us in our Top, Bottom, Middle, Dominant/Other groups need to agree that there are no simple answers to how we are to manage the conditions we are facing:

   as Tops, our responsibility for the system

   as Bottoms, our vulnerability in the system

   as Middles, our tearing

   and as Dominants and Others, the turbulence that develops as our cultures meet.

   There is nothing but uncertainty.

2. **See the possibilities emerging.** We need to recognize how in the presence of uncertainty we begin to experience possibilities, ways in which we *could* respond to the conditions we are facing. We need to understand that seeing possibilities is a reasonable way in which the mind responds to uncertainty. The unhelpful way the mind responds is to quickly transform these possibilities into positions of certainty.

3. **Avoid polarization.** We need to notice how quick we are to attach ourselves to positions and, once attached, to drive one another ever further into opposition.

4. **Hold possibilities up to the light.** We need to be able to hold our favored possibilities (before they harden into positions) up to the light, examining them from all sides, seeing limitations as well as

strengths. *If we don't deal with the down sides of our possibilities, we can be sure someone else will.* Treating possibilities this way, with all their complexities, enables us to consider a wider range of actions and cautions. Uncertainty calls for this kind of complexity.

5. **Use your flexibility.** We need to be able to see ourselves not as opinions but as complex differentiated systems capable of multiple approaches to the uncertainty we are facing.

6. **Be a Force for what is missing in your group.** We need to be able to free ourselves from positions and instead function as Forces; that is, to do what needs to be done whether or not it conforms within our comfort zones. As Forces, we are capable of becoming what is missing in our system's efforts to survive and develop.

From Rigid Position to Flexible Force

In the Top world, we may become a Force for expansion—*even though we are personally uncomfortable with change*—because we know that the survival of our system depends on expansion.

Similarly, in the Bottom world, we may become Forces for radical action—*again, even though that position makes us uncomfortable*—because we believe that without such action our group's survival is endangered.

We can be downward-aligned Middles, whose hearts are generally with our workers, but become Forces for confronting them because their actions threaten to weaken the system.

We can become Forces for preserve/protect not because we are wedded to that position but because we believe that members of our culture need to examine the consequences that the lack of that orientation is producing.

As Forces, we are not tied to habit or value or personal comfort; our focus is on our system, what is missing, and what is needed for its survival. As Forces, each of us will have come a long way from being that single-minded carrier of a fixed position to *each of us becoming a complex differentiated system, capable of responding complexly to the complex situations we face.*

From Antagonists to Team

It is possible for us to effect a remarkable transformation from conditions in which we have been battling with one another—causing personal stress, fractured relationships, and diminished organizational effectiveness—to conditions in which we are working together to deal constructively with the fundamental uncertainties of our positions.

Complex Teamwork in the Bottom Space

Let's see how this would work in the Bottom world, a world of vulnerability. Say that the Tops have come up with a new organizational change initiative. The message to Bottoms is that this new initiative is essential to keeping pace with the competition and key to organizational survival. *And* it's going to require some major changes by the Bottoms.

In the face of uncertainty, two opposing possibilities are immediately "in the air" in the Bottom world: protect ourselves by investing our energies in this new initiative, or protect ourselves by resisting this initiative. These two possibilities could readily harden into fixed positions that would fracture the Bottom group.

How It Could Go

The resisters could easily become the Hards and the investors the Softs. And the harder each pushed its position, the more firmly it would embed the other in its position.

Softs see investing in the new initiative as essential to managing their vulnerability (*If the company sinks, we all sink*); Hards see the key to survival in keeping Tops from taking advantage of them (*Invest all you want, they could still ship the jobs to China*). Hards see Softs as being naïve, easily taken advantage of by Tops. Softs see Hards as being unreasonably recalcitrant and, through their resistance, ensuring organizational failure. The split could then become complete.

What Else Is Possible?

If Hards and Softs could hold up their positions to the light, they would see the strengths and limitations of each. Soft can strengthen the system *and* still leave workers vulnerable to Top discretion. Hard could protect Bottoms against abuse *and*, by withholding effort, could jeopardize the system.

Rather than fighting with one another over which position is correct—both are, neither is—a teamwork approach would be to pursue a Hard/Soft strategy, one that takes into account the strengths and limitations of each approach. A strategy in which Bottoms work on survival by investing their energies in the survival of the system *and* work on survival by protecting themselves against Top abuse by pressing for the best working conditions and contractual arrangements they can get.

Such a strategy is feasible when possibilities are experienced as possibilities—responses to uncertainty—and not as answers. As such, they enable us to shape complex possibilities into complex strategies.

Such a view of possibilities enables any one of us to be a Force. *We do not need to be either the Good Worker or the Hard Negotiator; we can be both—investing our creative energies in the new change initiative and pressing for the best contractual arrangements we can get.*

Complex Possibilities Produce Complex Strategies

In the Top world, instead of Conservatives battling against and protecting themselves from Expansives, it is possible to zestfully pursue expansion while working with equal zest to cover the hazards of expansion. This becomes feasible once we see *expand* and *conserve* as possibilities—responses to uncertainty—and not as answers. As such, we are able to see and work with *both* the strengths *and* limitations of each. And as we move ahead with our strategy, we do not have to be a position pushing for *either* conserve *or* expand; each of us can be a Force for both directions.

Similar complex strategies are possible in dealing with the uncertainties in the Middle world and that of the Dominants and Others. The fundamental principles are (1) see possibilities as possibilities and not as answers, (2) explore the positives and negatives of possibilities, and (3) develop complex strategies that include multiple possibilities along with their strengths and limitations.

■　　■　　■

He: This idea of being a Force is intriguing.

She: In what way?

He: I always see myself as a firm Allow/Adapter—the kind-hearted one. And I guess I'm pretty righteous in my position and evaluative of those Preserve/Protectors—the bad ones.

She: So, what are you seeing now?

He: That I've never been able to face the down side of Allow/Adapt.

She: And it's there?

He: Oh sure. Allow/Adapt can also mean losing things I value in my culture; it may mean tolerating behavior I find offensive; it may mean my making believe that things are OK even when they're not; it may mean my feeling less at home in my own culture; it may mean having to deal with difficult issues and difficult people; it may mean being nostalgic for the good old days before the others showed up.

She: So what are you seeing now?

He: That I can be a Force instead of a position. That I can be an Allow/Adapt/Preserve/Protector.

She: Seeing both sides of allow/adapt or preserve/protect or any of the other possibilities can give you a more realistic and creative approach to the uncertainty you are facing.

He: My Allower/Adapter friends will see me as having gone conservative.

She: And the Preserver/Protectors will see you as a wishy-washy liberal. That's the price of dealing with the reality of uncertainty. The real question is, How will you now use this expanded sense of yourself as a Force in working with the meeting of cultures?

Scene 3
Facing and Escaping the Uncertainties of Existence

71 Not All Possibilities Are Possible

As described in "The Mystery of the Swim" (**3**), Barth's "swimmers" have not the foggiest notion of what their swim is about, yet this in no way limits their capacity to create multiple meanings for it and stories to explain it, all of which (if you haven't already figured this out) happen to be wrong. These stories are all possible responses to the present uncertainty, but the point is, none of these possibilities has merit. Barth is sending us a message not so much about these "swimmers" as about we humans and our capacity, in the face of the uncertainties in our lives, to create "possibilities" that explain them.

She: You can go too far with this flexible possibilities business.

He: What are you saying?

She: Not all possibilities are possible. Not all arguments are worth considering.

He: A bit more detail, please.

She: We have these huge brains, and one thing these brains are capable of is making up stories. Many of these stories—like those of Barth's "swimmers"—are simply not true, but we cling to them because in the condition of uncertainty they serve other purposes:

they make our lives more interesting,

they comfort us,

they justify greed and hating our enemies,

they provide meaning where no real meaning exists,

they ennoble us over others,

they make pain and loss endurable.

He: This seems like a good thing.

She: It is, except when it's not. Despite the stories certain brains have concocted and are committed to:

The holocaust did happen.

The CIA did not introduce AIDS into the black community.

The earth was not created five thousand years ago.

Evolution continues.

The Jews did not have advance warning of the bombing of the twin towers in New York City.

Furthermore, many, if not all of the events described in the Bible and the Koran and the Bhagavad Gita never happened.

Yet, for each of the above, there are people who have counter-vailing myths (stories, "possibilities") that they cling to because:

they make their lives more interesting,

they comfort them,

they justify them in hating their enemies,

they ennoble them over others,

they make pain and loss endurable.

He: Shouldn't we look for the merit in such stories?

She: *(angrily)* Not a merit worthy of debate. We have been exploring our human response to uncertainty, but certain situations are not uncertain. They are facts, verifiable events. Fruitless and pointless debates happen when people, for the above-mentioned reasons, argue on behalf of these possibilities that aren't really possible. However, just because our brains are capable of constructing self-serving explanations for which there is no support-ive evidence, this does not give us reason to search for some merit in these stories. These are not your opportunities for flexi-bility. There is no common ground to be sought.

He: These are myths; they are often beautiful myths. You're being unreasonable.

She: No, I am being reasonable, logical. Myths are unreasonable.

He: But they do have their place, don't they?

She: As long as they keep their place.

72 Coping with Uncertainty Through Mythos and Logos

There are two ways we find meaning in the presence of uncertainty: through mythos and logos—myth and logic. Stories are the instrument of myth, science the instrument of logic. Each exists in its own realm. In the realm of myth, there is no need for evidence of factuality; myth stands on its own with its potential to enrich our understanding of our human condition and aspirations. In the realm of logos, there is no room for myth; evidence rules. When mythos and logos are kept in their separate realms, there is no difficulty; we can be enriched by our myths without seeking or needing foundations in truth, and we can pursue science without concern for its conformity with myth.

It is when mythos and logos become one that confusion, tension, and real trouble develop.[3]

To some the Bible, the Veda, the Koran, the Kaballah, and the Bhagavad Gita are powerful myths whose stories enrich and guide their lives; they do not judge these books against the scientific standards of logos. For others, these books no longer exist solely in the realm of myth but rather exist in a realm in which mythos and logos are one. To them, these stories have become historical facts and unassailable truths. And too many of those who believe this will harass you, humiliate you, coerce you, try to convert you, banish you, and even kill you for stating otherwise.

A Myth I Can Live By

Several years ago, I was teaching at a leadership institute with a Buddhist spiritual underpinning.[4] A discussion arose among faculty as to the role of God in our work. The question of God grows out of the fundamental uncertainties of human existence: Who are we? How did we get here? Are we alone in the universe? How did the universe get to be the universe? Is there a purpose to our existence? Is there life after death? and so forth. Science (logos) attempts to investigate whichever of these questions is amenable to science, and leaves the rest to mythos. And mythos has not been lax in its treatment of these uncertainties—considering the many religions of the world and the hundreds of creation stories that have arisen in response to these mysteries.[5]

Although God has not been a central player in my work (as far as I can determine), that did not keep me from getting involved in the faculty conversation. To grasp my "theology," one needs to understand the part puzzles play in my life.

While some rise before the sun to do their daily prayers, I head off each morning to my local coffee shop and the *New York Times* crossword puzzle; the tension builds over the week as, day by day, the puzzles grow progressively trickier and more difficult, and my day cannot proceed until the day's puzzle is solved. Puzzles are also at the core of my work: in this book and other writings I work at unlocking the mysteries of organizational life; how come it goes the way it usually goes, and what else is possible? And, in my work as Power Lab anthropologist, I search for all parts of the story and try to assemble them like pieces in a jigsaw puzzle until the whole picture comes clear.

So, in the best tradition of seeing God in our own image, my God is the Great Puzzle Maker, and my work lies in trying to solve some piece of the Grand Puzzle, to contribute to the unraveling of the whole. I have good company in this quest: Albert Einstein spoke of trying to understand the mind of God; he spoke of great scientists as people who stand in "rapturous amazement at the harmony of natural law." This harmony is not always beautiful; quite often, its consequences are ugly. I have, for example, written about the Terrible Dance of Power in which one group has a vision of a better world (through fascism, communism, manifest destiny, Christianity, Islam, a new world order, or some other such inspiration), only to find some *Them* who stand in the way of this vision, and then a predictable story unfolds, like a dance, of oppression, death, and destruction. There is a terrible beauty to this story as possibilities morph into positions, factions arise, harden in their positions, and interplay with one another—moderates and radicals, gradualists and extremists, liberals and conservatives—escalating from disagreement to debate to confrontation to minor skirmishes to colossal destruction.

So we get to the ultimate uncertainty. Is there a god who allows such terrible things to happen? What kind of a god is that? Does that god have a point? Is he or she or it teaching us a lesson? Or do these terrible things happen because there is no god?

Many people throughout the ages have offered answers to these questions. Forgive me (many of you won't), but I say nobody really knows. Nobody. It's all uncertainty, a huge unfathomable uncertainty into which flows our richest myth-making.

So here is my myth. In my myth, God, in whatever manner inconceivable to me, gave us a powerful gift: the possibility of awareness and choice, but just the possibility; and then God retreated from the world and has not been heard from since. Whatever else has transpired is the result of how we have handled or botched that gift.

Organizational life may seem to some to be a relatively barren locale for spiritual growth; it is, however, rich with opportunity. So much can go wrong. "Stuff" happens: unwanted complications come your way; the service you've been waiting for is long delayed and when it does comes it is unsatisfactory; your working conditions are poor and "they" are not fixing them; try as you might, you don't seem able to satisfy anyone—this one is angry at you, that one is disappointed, and the other one is not paying you the attention you feel you deserve. So many opportunities. When these conditions hit, it is as if we are standing before two doors: Door A and Door B. Door A would take us into our Tunnel of Limited Options and Door B would take us to higher possibilities for ourselves and our systems. It seems like a simple enough choice, but right away there is a problem: We don't see any doors and we don't experience any choice; instead, we go blindly through Door A, falling into fixed positions and opinions, falling into alienation, territoriality, and groupthink, sucking up responsibility to ourselves and away from others, whining and complaining, falling into the Side Show, making up stories in which we are either the hero or the victim, taking revenge, doing less than our best, comforting ourselves in righteousness, diminishing ourselves, diminishing the quality of our relationships with others, diminishing our contributions to our organization and to the world.

In my myth, the beginning of spirituality, and the solution to the puzzle, come with the awareness of Door A: when we step out of the Tunnel of Limited Options, when we become aware of our condition, when we see that door not as the way things are but as a choice. And then there is Door B. Stepping through that door, we abandon all victimhood and righteousness; we accept and work with uncertainty; we experience ourselves not as fixed positions but as flexible Forces; we accept responsibility for our condition and for the condition of our systems; we accept our place as cocreators of these conditions. When we go through Door B—how can I say it?—we become better beings in and of ourselves, in our relationships with others, and in our contributions to our organization and the world.

Every day, and throughout each day, organizational life gives us countless opportunities for spirituality: to be aware and to choose. So that has been my puzzle. Why are we built this way, with both reflexive blindness along with its negative consequences and the possibility of awareness and choice? And who or what built us this way? The great Puzzle Maker?

One final note about my god:

I will not kill anyone in the name of this god, nor would I try

to convert you to believe in this god;

but I do believe that this is a god worth living by.

He: Do you believe in this God?

Barry: Are you asking me about mythos or logos?

SUMMARY

In this section, we have explored the fundamental uncertainties underlying many of the situations we regularly face in organizational life. We have seen how our reflexive escapes from uncertainty into certainty limit us personally—the scope and depth of our *being*—and how they limit the potential contributions we can make from whatever positions we are in. We have also seen how this reflexive escape into certainty leads us into unnecessary and destructive battles with one another—firm positions in opposition to firm positions. And we have explored the possibilities of accepting uncertainty, living in it, and working with the challenges it offers, becoming flexible Forces—rather than fixed positions—in the service of greater personal contribution, constructive group relationships, and increased organizational power.

And, finally, we have peeked into the fundamental awesome uncertainty of human existence and our efforts to find meaning in the face of that uncertainty.

The Next Act—Seeing More

She: So, can you see systems now?

He: Well, I think so, and I'm amazed at what I see. I'm becoming aware of the stories I make up. I find myself wondering about the history of events: What led up to this moment? I'm constantly seeing myself in relationship with others—as a Top or a Bottom, an End or a Middle, a Provider or a Customer. I'm more aware of Turf and Alienation and GroupThink. I'm beginning to see how processes get politicized. I'm coming to face the uncertainty underlying unquestioned beliefs. I see quite a bit.

She: You see the dances?

He: I sure do. And I see that I can change them. And I know that it's not always easy, that there are plenty of opportunities to retreat into the old dances.

She: And resistance?

He: The sound of the old dance shaking.

She: Still, you seem puzzled.

He: I see quite a bit, yet I'm still struck by how much I don't see.

She: Ah, but that is such an important beginning! It leads you to question your experiences, and that is critical if we are to stop our misguided battles with one another.

He: I think I understand, but say more.

She: We are like Barth's "swimmers." We are in our own night-sea journey. We are Burdened and we blame circumstances. We are Oppressed and we blame higher-ups. We are Torn and we blame our jobs. We are Alienated from others, or locked into territorial struggles with them, or caught up in fantasies of our group's superiority, feeling certain that our experiences of others and ourselves are grounded in reality. We dominate others, unaware that we are doing so. We hate others and oppress them, assured that our feelings and actions are justified. All of this happens because we do not question the validity of our experiences.

We do not see the swim we are in, we do not understand its

meaning, nor do we see how our experiences are shaped by the form and function of that swim. Without that "seeing" we are at the mercy of the swim.

He: You said something else just now, something about the meaning of the swim. Until now we have not talked about meaning. Are you saying that you know the meaning of the swim we are in?

She: Maybe I do.

He: And?

She: It is a test.

He: Of what?

She: A test of our humanity. It is a test of our ability to move to a new level of possibility for ourselves as human beings. Blind reflex has taken a terrible toll; some of the damage has been minor, some catastrophic: misunderstanding, hate, disappointment, lost opportunities, oppression, destruction. And we humans show no lack of capacity for continuing along that path.

And then there is this other path, more difficult to discern; we are unclear where it leads, hesitant to take the first step. And rightly so. That first step requires great humility. Maybe, in our system blindness, we have been wrong about these others; maybe, in sliding into one dance or the other, we have misjudged them. Maybe it was great folly for us to hate these others, fear them, separate ourselves from them, escape from them, avoid them, dominate them, hurt them, oppress them, maybe even destroy them. Maybe, instead of falling out of partnership, we could have created great Top, Middle, and Bottom teams. Maybe we didn't have to suppress one another's cultures or tolerate one another; maybe we could have created something special. Maybe it was all a terrible mistake. And maybe we are still doing it.

So that is the test. To see systems or be blind to them. The costs of blindness are clear. Who knows what possibilities "seeing" holds for us?

He: That's quite a test.

She: The good news is, it's a test we can take every day.

Epilogue: A Continuing Revolution

Seeing Systems is more than a book; it is a mission, the goal of which is to fundamentally transform they way we experience our lives in social systems. This book is a beginning, but the successful completion of the mission is a ways off. Consider the following example:

A colleague recently described a painful relationship issue involving two partners. By now, this will be a familiar story to you. The two are codirectors (Tops) of an international social change agency. Both are well-known and well-respected in their fields; both are authors of best-selling books; both are experts in helping people understand and work effectively with one another. Yet *their* relationship is fraying and on the edge of dissolution. The partners have different orientations regarding how they do their work; until recently, this was considered not a problem but a strength of the organization. Of late, that has changed. Now

- One partner insists that his orientation is the *right* way.

- One partner does not feel respected for his contributions; in fact, he feels regularly belittled by the other partner.

- One partner says he no longer trusts the other partner.

- One partner does not feel supported by the other.

- There is such bitterness in the relationship that it is difficult to engage in rational conversation.

What we have here is another in an apparently limitless line of failures of partnership in the Top world: a failure to understand and manage that space of complexity and accountability, along with the assumption that since we are good, intelligent people, that ought to be enough to ensure success. Then follow the predictable consequences of both functional and directional differentiation reminiscent of Edgar and Charles (see **40**, "The Success of a Business, the Failure of Its Partners").

But the partners are not experiencing this breakdown as a systemic issue; to them it feels painfully personal. Rather than understanding and managing the top systemic space, they are in its grips, which captures the continuing challenge of this work: to shift the dominant world view from the personal to the systemic. Simply stated, much that feels personal is not personal. We are systems creatures. Our consciousness—

how we experience ourselves, others, our systems, and other systems—is shaped by the structure and processes of the systems we are in. Our failure to recognize this fundamental connection comes at costs ranging from simple misunderstandings to severely diminished organizational effectiveness to horrendous human catastrophes. With system sight we have greater leverage for avoiding those costs and creating more sane social systems in which to live, grow, and contribute.

Pathways to System Sight

In this section I'll be describing some of the processes currently in use in this mission to transform system blindness into system sight. If this mission captures your passion, I welcome your involvement.

A Differentiated/Homogenized Strategy

To transform hard-wired personal world views into a systemic one will require a richly complex (differentiated) strategy. For some people the written word will suffice, others need the direct experience; some need the science, others the humor; some require the full detail, for others the requirement is *keep it short*! So our intention is to pursue a multifaceted approach that allows all to find their way.

Underlying the variety in approaches is the strategy they all hold in common (homogenization). The key to attaining system sight lies in confronting people with familiar experiences that feel very personal to them or, specific to their organizations, or both. And then to have them recognize that those experiences are not about them and not about their organizations. To paraphrase Leonard Cohen, that's the crack that lets the light in.[1] It is that Aha! experience we seek to create, by whatever means.

The following are some of the tools currently available for letting in the light; others are being developed, and still others remain to be created.

The written word. This book, and the written word generally,[2] have that possibility for transformation. Through the cases and the dances and the concepts, we see the familiar and recognize that it's not about us. One reader captured well our fondest wish for the power of the written word. She talked about stepping into a situation long familiar to her and, having immersed herself in this framework, being hit by "a tidal wave of understanding." A tidal wave of understanding. Seeing the old with a powerful new set of lenses that transforms one's experience and opens up avenues for more effective action. That's the possibility of the written word. And, reader, if you find value in these systemic lenses, I encourage you to pass them on to others.

Experiential programs. If you or your organization or client want to move from the written word to the playing field, the **Organization Workshop** and **Power Lab** continue to be high-energy media for generating system sight through their combination of direct involvement in the action, reflection, TOOTs, and system frameworks. Envision an organization in which, throughout, there is common language and understanding of the worlds of Tops, Middles, Bottoms, and Customers; where there are illuminating workshop stories to share; where people recognize the Side Show and the Center Ring; where they are familiar with the Dance of Blind Reflex and the Tunnel of Limited Options; where they can work together as flexible Forces; where they see choices in themselves and others; where they are more likely to avoid the pitfalls of system blindness and instead choose to create more productive outcomes for themselves and their systems.

Trainers. There is a growing network of Organization Workshop trainers across the United States, Canada, the United Kingdom, Portugal, South Africa, Australia, and India who are bringing this work—through high-impact programs—to organizations across the globe.[3] You may want to explore whether this is a network you'd like to be part of.

Documentary. *Power Lab: Living in New Hope* takes the viewer into the life of a single Power Lab: Tops (Elite), Middles (Managers), and Bottoms (Immigrants) engaged in intensive interaction. *Power Lab* gives the viewer an emotional and intellectual experience of societal and organizational issues—issues that regularly unfold in Top, Middle, and Bottom groups and across class line. My commentary provides the systemic lens that sheds new light on familiar system dynamics. The documentary is an eye-opening experience for students of social system life.

Systemic Presentations are powerful tools for generating system sight. They can create that Aha! experience for the client: *The presentations are describing us, but they don't know us, so something else must be going on here.*

- *How Come It Goes the Way It Usually Goes* shows how, despite the best intentions all around, organizations keep falling into the same old dysfunctional scenarios.

- *Top Teams* demonstrates how Top teams, though assembled with great promise, all too often fall into turf issues, with destructive consequences for the members and their organizations.

- *Middle Power* describes how Middles regularly become alienated from one another, with negative consequences for themselves and their systems.

Each of these presentations describes a familiar scenario—*not yours but a lot like yours*—with the predictable dysfunctional consequences of system blindness, and it describes the individual and system power that comes with system sight. Check www.powerandsystems.com for the availability of th se and other presentations.

Human Systems Coaching. Take a leaf from "His Magic Consultant Card," while keeping all of "Her" cautions in mind. Incorporate this human systems framework into your individual and group coaching. Start with yourself, then move on to others. Help people change from what is, for many, a pervasive personal bias to a systemic understanding of the situations they and others are facing. Help them understand and work with the fundamental uncertainty underlying the conflicts they are in; help them become aware of their systemic relationships and where the responsibility dance is taking them; help them to notice the Side Shows they are in and how to move to the Center Ring. Help them to grasp the basic point: *Much that seems personal is not personal.*

Stage Performances is a way of bringing the system perspective to a broader audience, those who might not read the books or who are unlikely candidates for the workshops. Two full-length theater pieces are now part of the Seeing Systems repertoire; others are in the works.

- *What a Way to Make a Living* is a three-act play in which Tops,

Middles, and Bottoms, with the help of a hard-hitting angel—a carrier of system sight—struggle to overcome the lures of the Dance of Blind Reflex and find their ways to partnership.

■ *Hierarchy* follows a charismatic leader whose success in transforming a demoralized, dysfunctional workforce runs into a conservative backlash that threatens to destroy all that he has created.

If this combination of theater and systems education captures your passion, check out the plays and articles at www.powerandsystems.com and contact us about staging them.[4]

The Terrible Dance of Power is a dramatic piece that has transformed people's experiences of human catastrophes ranging from the holocaust to the Cambodian and Rwanda genocides to the Iraq war. The dance always begins with people in power seeing themselves as the bearers of some higher mission—Manifest Destiny, The Master Race, The One True Religion, The Way—and standing in their way, the "others." And then the catastrophe unfolds until the higher mission inevitably turns to dust. Once again, the dance takes what appears to be events tied to a specific set of circumstances and casts them in a systemic light. *The Terrible Dance of Power* has been staged and treated to dramatic readings, and it has been passed from person to person in hotspots throughout the world. It is available as a downloadable PDF at www.powerandsystems.com.

Staging Performances is a way of involving organization members in rehearsing and ultimately performing these organizational plays. In the rehearsal process the actors develop system sight through immersion in their roles, and through the performances they share that gift with others.

The **Internet** offers additional avenues to spread the message in humorous as well as serious ways through blogs, systemic analyses of current events, viral messages, videos, theater pieces, animation, and other technologies yet to be developed. "Empowering Accountability" was our first entry in the viral world; it is available on our website. If you feel it can bring humor and comfort to other long-suffering Middles, be sure to pass it on.[5]

And for those who value the science, I recommend my pamphlet **"There Is No New Scientific Paradigm . . . Yet (Toward A Most Practical Science of Social System Life),"**[6] in which I make the case that (1) despite frequent references to paradigms and paradigm shifts in the management and organization literature, there are no new paradigms in the sense that Thomas Kuhn described them in his landmark essay,[7] and (2) the framework presented here *is* a legitimate candidate for paradigm status, one from which research extending, elaborating, testing, and applying the framework follows naturally. It's a position we can debate in the best scientific tradition.

An Individuated/Integrated Strategy

The foregoing are directions Power + Systems is taking in the pursuit of this Seeing Systems mission. Then there is you. You are welcome to join us in any of these strategies, and I encourage you to develop your own direction. What unique skills, interest, technologies can you bring to this mission? Individuation is welcome; all that I ask is that you keep all of us informed so that we are all strengthened by one another— that's the integration piece. Together we can participate in this continuing revolution to bring increased understanding and sanity to the many systems of our lives.

Barry Oshry
August 2007

Notes

Prologue

1. The evolution of the Power Lab and many of the lessons I have learned from it are described in *Leading Systems: Lessons from the Power Lab*. San Francisco: Berrett-Koehler, 1999.

2. The Craigville Conference Center sits atop a bluff overlooking beautiful Nantucket Sound. For information, write to Craigville Conference Center, 39 Prospect Avenue, Craigville, MA 02632. Telephone: 508-775-1265.

3. *The Terrible Dance of Power* dramatizes one such dance that regularly leads to wholesale death and destruction, invariably in the name of great and noble causes. This dance has had many dramatic readings and performances and has been circulated around the world. A PDF can be downloaded from www.powerandsystems.com.

4. Barry Oshry, *The Dance of Disempowerment*. Boston: Power + Systems, 1992.

Act One

1. John Barth, "Night-Sea Journey." In *Lost in the Funhouse*. New York: Doubleday, 1968.

2. If you want to know the meaning behind the night-sea journey, go to www.powerandsystems.com. There you will find *my* meaning of the Swim. Be forewarned: although I feel certain that my story is *the* story, it may be just another story.

3. *October Project*, unpublished anthropologist report, Power + Systems, 1986.

Act Two

1. A briefer version of the Daniel case was presented in *In the Middle*. Boston: Power + Systems, Inc., 1994.

Act Three

1. This same experience of seeing the whole was described in Act One in "History's Burst of Illumination." In *Leading Systems: Lessons from the*

Power Lab, I describe a different, yet equally powerful example of a burst of system seeing. See "Epilogue: An Experiment That Did Not Fail."

2. Lewis Thomas, *The Lives of a Cell*. New York: Viking, 1974.

3. Richard Parker, *John Kenneth Galbraith: His Life, His Politics, His Economics*. New York: Farrar, Straus & Giroux, 2005.

4. I cite the *possibility* of systematic differences based on my reading of the following:

   Carol Gilligan, *In a Different Voice*. Cambridge: Harvard University Press, 1982. Gilligan poses a distinct female orientation to morality, one that reflects the importance of what I would call integrative concerns—connection, interdependencies, caring, and responsibility.

   Deborah Tannen, *You Just Don't Understand*. New York: Random House, 1990. Tannen points to consistent differences in male/female communication patterns, differences that are consistent with individuating/integrating tendencies: Men, being more competitive, try to avoid being one-down; women, being inclined to preserve intimacy, avoid conflict.

   Robert May, *Sex and Fantasy*. New York: Norton, 1980. May's research points to consistent gender differences, again consistent with individuation and integration: males being more likely to function in detached, isolated fashion in solitary work. *Rational, independent,* and *objective* are words May uses to describe the positive side of the male tendency; he uses the words *cold, detached,* and *unfeeling* to describe the negative side. May writes, "Women have less of a penchant for deciding things independent of the relevant network of connections. . . . They put a faithfulness to human ties above dedication to 'principle' or pure 'independence' of judgment."

   David Bakan, *The Duality of Human Existence*. Boston: Beacon Press, 1966. Balkan cites research demonstrating consistent male/female differences in "agency" (interchangeable with individuation) and "communion" (interchangeable with integration).

Act IV

1. Chapter 4, "Begging with Barry," in *Leading Systems: Lessons from the Power Lab*.

2. *Power Lab: Living in New Hope*, a 105-minute prize-winning documentary written and directed by Allan Kobernick of Blue Sky Productions. Power + Systems, Boston.

3. See particularly *The Battle for God* by Karen Armstrong. New York: Random House, 2000.
4. The Shambhala Institute for Authentic Leadership conducts a yearly summer program in Halifax, Nova Scotia, Canada, combining ancient meditative teachings and practices with the work of leading-edge thinkers in the field of social change. www.shambhalainstitute.org.
5. Enter "creation myths" in any search engine and you will find rich tales of how all that we know came to be; certain sites also offer thoughtful analyses of these myths. One that led me on several interesting trails is www.mythinglinks.org.

Epilogue
1. "Anthem," words and music by Leonard Cohen.
2. Additional publications dealing with this human systems framework are described at www.powerandsystems.com.
3. For Organization Workshop trainers in your area, call 1-800-241-0598.
4. Plays and articles on organization theater can be found at www.powerandsystems .com.
5. "Empowering Accountability" can be found at www.powerandsystems.com. If you feel it can ease the pain of other suffering Middles, do pass it on.
6. "There Is No New Paradigm . . . Yet (Toward A Most Practical Science of Social System Life)." Boston: Power + Systems, 2000. The pamphlet is available as a downloadable PDF at www.powerandsystems.com
7. Thomas S. Kuhn, *The Structure of Scientific Revolutions*, third edition. Chicago: University of Chicago Press, 1996.

DBR   p.64   Dance of Blind Reflex

Toot

p. 119
   121 - 24

p. 138

About the Author

For over forty years, Barry Oshry has been on a single-minded quest to unlock the mysteries of power and powerlessness in social systems. Throughout his career he has created organizational and societal simulations that have served as both learning environments for participants and research laboratories for himself. He began his work in the 1960s at Boston University, where he developed large-scale organizational simulations for undergraduates in business. Throughout the 1960s, Oshry continued his research at the university and at the National Training Laboratories' Management Work Conferences and Community Laboratories.

In 1970, he created the Power Lab, which continues to attract executives, managers, educators, and consultants from across the globe. The Power Lab is the subject of a prize-winning documentary, Power Lab: Living in New Hope, written and directed by Allan Kobernick.

In his writings, Oshry often deals with serious issues in nontraditional ways, "the dance" being one of his most prevalent metaphors. His essay "The Terrible Dance of Power," and book "The Dance of Disempowerment" have been the basis of theatrical productions by the Seattle Public Theatre and the Seattle Mime Company, and there have been numerous dramatic readings of his works.

In recent years, Oshry has extended his work into the arena of staged performance; in addition to his full-length plays, his ten-minute play Peace, which deals with the Israeli/Palestinian issue as played out in the tension between father and daughter, has been performed in numerous play festivals.

Oshry is married to Karen Ellis Oshry, who has been his partner and collaborator in all ventures for over thirty years–from waiting on tables to theory development to gourmet dining to conducting workshops around the world. Karen has been the first reader of all his writings. She is a sharp observer of systems, a tough critic, an empowering coach, a cosufferer in the hard times, and a cocelebrant in the good ones. The Oshrys enjoy the friendship of two children, their spouses, and two grandchildren.

In 1975, the Oshrys founded Power + Systems, Inc., a not-for-profit educational corporation, whose staff continues to offer the Power

Lab, the Organization Workshop, and the Merging Cultures Workshop to organizations and institutions around the globe.

Barry Oshry can be reached at barry@powerandsystems.com. www.powerandsystems.com

Berrett–Koehler
Publishers

Berrett-Koehler is an independent publisher dedicated to an ambitious mission: *Creating a World That Works for All*.

We believe that to truly create a better world, action is needed at all levels—individual, organizational, and societal. At the individual level, our publications help people align their lives with their values and with their aspirations for a better world. At the organizational level, our publications promote progressive leadership and management practices, socially responsible approaches to business, and humane and effective organizations. At the societal level, our publications advance social and economic justice, shared prosperity, sustainability, and new solutions to national and global issues.

A major theme of our publications is "Opening Up New Space." Berrett-Koehler titles challenge conventional thinking, introduce new ideas, and foster positive change. Their common quest is changing the underlying beliefs, mindsets, institutions, and structures that keep generating the same cycles of problems, no matter who our leaders are or what improvement programs we adopt.

We strive to practice what we preach—to operate our publishing company in line with the ideas in our books. At the core of our approach is stewardship, which we define as a deep sense of responsibility to administer the company for the benefit of all of our "stakeholder" groups: authors, customers, employees, investors, service providers, and the communities and environment around us.

We are grateful to the thousands of readers, authors, and other friends of the company who consider themselves to be part of the "BK Community." We hope that you, too, will join us in our mission.

A BK Business Book

This book is part of our BK Business series. BK Business titles pioneer new and progressive leadership and management practices in all types of public, private, and nonprofit organizations. They promote socially responsible approaches to business, innovative organizational change methods, and more humane and effective organizations.

Berrett–Koehler
Publishers

A community dedicated to creating
a world that works for all

Visit Our Website: www.bkconnection.com

Read book excerpts, see author videos and Internet movies, read our authors' blogs, join discussion groups, download book apps, find out about the BK Affiliate Network, browse subject-area libraries of books, get special discounts, and more!

Subscribe to Our Free E-Newsletter, the *BK Communiqué*

Be the first to hear about new publications, special discount offers, exclusive articles, news about bestsellers, and more! Get on the list for our free e-newsletter by going to **www.bkconnection.com**.

Get Quantity Discounts

Berrett-Koehler books are available at quantity discounts for orders of ten or more copies. Please call us toll-free at (800) 929-2929 or email us at **bkp.orders@aidcvt.com**.

Join the BK Community

BKcommunity.com is a virtual meeting place where people from around the world can engage with kindred spirits to create a world that works for all. **BKcommunity.com** members may create their own profiles, blog, start and participate in forums and discussion groups, post photos and videos, answer surveys, announce and register for upcoming events, and chat with others online in real time. Please join the conversation!